THE ESSENCE OF
SPIRITUAL RELIGION

THE ESSENCE OF SPIRITUAL RELIGION

D. ELTON TRUEBLOOD

"The humble, meek, merciful, just, pious, and devout souls, are everywhere of one religion; and when death has taken off the mask, they will know one another, though the diverse liveries they wear here make them strangers."

William Penn, *Fruits of Solitude*

HARPER & ROW, PUBLISHERS

New York, Evanston, San Francisco, London

FIRST HARPER & ROW PAPERBACK EDITION PUBLISHED IN 1975.

ISBN: 0-06-068576-x

LIBRARY OF CONGRESS CATALOG CARD NUMBER: 74-7684

To

RUFUS MATTHEW JONES

Contents

		PAGE
	PREFACE TO THE PAPERBACK EDITION	ix
I.	THE NATURE OF RELIGION IN GENERAL	1
II.	SPIRITUAL RELIGION AND BELIEF	18
III.	THE SPIRITUAL INWARDNESS OF JESUS	29
IV.	THE SPIRITUAL NATURE OF GOD	41
V.	THE SPIRITUAL NATURE OF MAN	53
VI.	SPIRITUAL SALVATION	63
VII.	WORSHIP IN SPIRIT AND IN TRUTH	74
VIII.	THE EXTENSION OF THE SACRAMENTAL	85
IX.	THE CONTINUITY OF REVELATION	98
X.	THE BASIS OF SPIRITUAL AUTHORITY	110
XI.	THE ABOLITION OF THE LAITY	128
XII.	THE IMPLICATIONS OF REVERENCE	142
	INDEX	155

This volume, now republished, was written in the summer of 1935 while I was Acting Dean of the Chapel of Harvard University. The book was accepted by the House of Harper, but the original printing was soon exhausted, and, because I was concentrating on other literary productions, I made no effort to keep it in print. Now the firm which has published all of my books in this country has graciously proposed reissuing, after a lapse of forty years, my first major effort. Though only a few changes have been made in the text—these being minor corrections—it seems right that a new preface should be added.

What is appropriate now is some consideration of the spiritual climate of forty years ago in contrast to our own in the seventies. In the summer of 1935 the great depression had not come to an end and we had to be very careful with finances. My Harvard salary for the entire summer session amounted to only a few hundred dollars. The students were serious and daily attendance at chapel was so good that sometimes every seat in Appleton Chapel was filled. With no evidence of student unrest, the Harvard Yard was a peaceful scene and I was able to write every day in Memorial Church without either tension or disturbance.

Today many elements of the general mood are radically different. Though the peak of the academic crisis was passed four years ago, we are still aware of turmoil every day, the voices on every side being far more clamorous than they were when I wrote my first book. We have moved into a far more stormy period of human history, and there is little prospect that the storm will subside. While there is more affluence, and while ordinary incomes are higher, even after discounting inflation, there is far more bitterness of spirit. The judgmental stance is now almost univeral, whereas four decades ago it appeared in only a segment of the population.

So far as religious experience is concerned, the supreme paradox of our time is that of the combination of obvious spiritual need with the failure to provide reasonable answers. It is part of our contemporary tragedy that, just when the world is becoming more aware of its need, the Church is becoming less sure of its mission. The Church today is confused regarding its true mission, often moving off into bizarre and marginal developments, the major reason for failure in mission being a diminished confidence in the message. It is difficult to think of anything more pertinent than a clear understanding of the meaning and truth of spiritual religion.

There is no parable in the Gospels which applies to our time more obviously than does that of the empty house. The house which is emptied, said Jesus, cannot *remain* empty; it is a law of life that a spiritual vacuum cannot be maintained. It will be occupied in one way or another, what comes in being possibly worse than that which has been discarded. Since the idea that change necessarily means progress is obviously fatuous, the truth of Christ's parable is demonstrated on every side. The popular interest in the occult, for much of which there is no rational justification whatever, is one of the many evidences of the truth which the parable represents.

One of the worst of our current intellectual dangers is in regard to time. We tend to suppose, uncritically, that what is a few years old is, for that reason, obsolete. We ask of a book not whether what is said is true but when it was written. The result of limitation to the passing moment is bound to be superficiality. One of the deepest of all lessons of history is that the truth of any proposition is independent of the time of its production. Consequently, the words of Socrates are not dimmed in the least by the fact that they were spoken twenty-four hundred years ago. In spite of changes in mood, I am convinced that the emphasis on spiritual religion, which I sought to make forty years ago, is valid today. This is the chief reason why I am grateful to my publishers for their decision to make these chapters available to a new generation, most of whom have never seen any part of my first book.

D.E.T.

I. The Nature of Religion in General

It is the purpose of this book to describe a particular type of religion which we are historically justified in calling "spiritual." This is not the religion of any one sect, but has appeared within all sects and outside all sects. Religion, so far as we know, is indigenous to man as man, but religion has taken on many forms of widely different value. Some religions have been definitely harmful in many respects and most religions have been overlaid with deposits of superstition and materialism. Our task is to look beneath this accumulated mass and discover, if we can, the genuine religion of the spirit which has existed in all generations.

That which is eventually described is not the result of an eclectic process. Our tool is not the pestle for the mixing of ingredients, but rather the scalpel by means of which the superfluous is carved away until the core of spiritual religion is displayed in its purity. This spiritual religion was already implicit in the dim beginnings of the religious tradition and has never been entirely lost in spite of the elements of magic, lust, and cruelty which have continually threatened to crush it. The student of the history and literature of religion is struck inevitably by the remarkable unity in the deepest insights of religious prophets and seers. The men to whom people in all ages have listened with respect in regard to the inner life have been in far closer agreement with one another than have their followers with each other.

It is not contended that the religion described in these pages is identical with the actual religion of any individual person any more than the ideal state is identical with any existent state. This spiritual religion has, however, been approximated by many and realized fleetingly by others. In one sense it has been a promise and in another a realized fact. Some who have not espoused it openly or consciously, have shown by their lives that this was indeed their true faith. For example, many specifically reject in words the notion of a continuous and immediate revelation and, at the same time, give evidence, in numerous concrete ways, that continuous revelation is a reality to them, the thing by which they really live. Thus we

2

must adopt the critical method of philosophy in going beyond the words of men, which are often mutually inconsistent, to their deeper core of faith.

If we attempt to make a short and simple definition of what we mean by the word "spiritual" we are not likely to be successful. It does not seem possible to define it without circularity, but circularity may be inherent in all definition. The study of logic is not a completely vain pursuit if it makes us realize that the problem of definition is much less simple than the uninitiated suppose. It is instructive to note that Auguste Sabatier's well-known attempts at the introduction of precise meaning into "spirit" and "spiritual" were not markedly successful.[1]

The real meaning of spiritual as used here will become clear in the following pages which are devoted to the description of the type of religion which the word is used to designate. Pending this full description, however, we may say in advance what some of the opposites or near-opposites of the term are. We are using spiritual as roughly opposed to *formal, literal, legal, ceremonial, hierarchical, sacerdotal, creedal, material, external, traditional,* but in each case qualifications will

[1] Auguste Sabatier, *Religions of Authority and the Religion of the Spirit.* London, 1904, pp. 281 *ff*.

3

be introduced. As the different chapters will show, spiritual religion is by no means *completely* antiformal or anticreedal. It certainly is not completely antiauthoritarian, and perhaps the weakest element in Sabatier's structure is his emphasis on authoritarianism as the chief center of opposition to spiritual religion. All this, however, will come out in what follows. We may say now that "spiritual religion" is shorthand for an entire ideational and emotional complex which requires a book for description. That is why the book has been written.

In our description of this type of religion which is at once unique and yet universal we shall have to inquire concerning those insights which are essential to the completed picture and shall ask further what conclusions these central insights entail. Our task is to present spiritual religion as a self-consistent system, a coherent view of the mysterious world in which we find ourselves. But before we turn to our picture of spiritual religion in particular, we must first understand something of the nature of religion in general.

If this good green earth were actually visited by the Man from Mars or any other extraterrestrial tourist the visitor would certainly find it hard to understand the reason for churches. Presumably he could understand the laboratories because

4

he could see that they are the sources of practical inventions and discoveries which change the general manner of living. He might understand our great legislative and administrative halls, for any social life demands government. He would surely understand the reason for our far-flung school system, since that system produces tangible results, at least in the increase of literacy. But how could we explain the churches? The difficulty of doing so is well expressed is some well-known words from the pen of Professor Pratt:

> Is it not a bit surprising that once in every seven days a great city should stop its work, and that half the population should turn out in their best clothes to hear one of their number read from a big book passages which most of them have long known almost by heart, that they should partake of bread and wine together, and (most astonishing of all) that they should all shut their eyes and listen while the man in the pulpit talks to someone who obviously is not there?[2]

The churches would, in all probability, be continuing mysteries to our visitor because they create no new physical products, the men in charge of them seem to be somewhat removed from the ordinary course of life, and, finally, it would often seem that the moral standards of those who visit

[2] James Bissett Pratt, *The Religious Consciousness.* New York, The Macmillan Co., 1920, p. 257.

5

the churches are in no way different from the moral standards of those who do not attend. If we explain to our interplanetary visitor that the churches are built for the sake of religion, he will want to know what we mean by religion, and what then shall we say?

Our answer to the person who asks about religion will be extremely difficult and may be impossible if the person is really a complete stranger to human ways. The meaning of religion takes us to the heart of the problem of the nature of man and the nature of the universe and, for this reason, no simple answer is ever sufficient. Many books present collections of short definitions of religion, but all are unsatisfactory because they *are* short, and because the mystery of life is long.

The easiest way to begin with our answer is to start with the fact that man does not live by bread alone. Man is a curious creature with curious needs, a creature who is not satisfied merely by food, much as he likes it, nor by sexual gratification, much as he craves it. The history of man's life can be understood as a story of the emergence of new desires and the consequent attempt to satisfy them. Man is not satisfied merely to produce a building which will protect him from the weather; he goes on to decorate his building and lovingly arranges the details of the structure so that they have what he calls a harmonious relationship to each other and to the whole. An ugly building will keep off the rain and snow as perfectly as will a beautiful building and may give the builder less trouble, but we constantly *take the trouble*.

Our language likewise is a monument to our curious needs. We have a practical use for language in that it makes us able to carry on joint enterprises with efficiency, but we do not leave our language at this level. We go on to refine this instrument of exchange until we produce a medium which carries fine shades of meaning from one person to another. We care, not only about what we say, but about the way we say it, and the result is great poetry. Poetry is as far removed from the simple command of the herd leader as a temple is removed from a stone hut, and we are creatures who need both poetry and temples. It is instructive to note that even the persons who live in poor structures are not happy until they find ways to beautify them. There is much to be learned from the fact that behind many small windows on dingy streets there are flowers growing in painted tomato cans.

Along with the curious desire for harmonious

decoration and the equally curious desire for delicately turned words and phrases is the desire to be *worthy*. Men of all generations have been willing to forego pleasures and give up many physical satisfactions because of loyalty to a mode of life with which these pleasures would not combine. In this strange desire to be worthy men have made a great distinction between *being* worthy and being *thought* worthy by others. A good argument can be made for the proposition that the most important single fact about man's life is the fact that he understands and cares about the distinction between praise and praiseworthiness. In every generation there have been prophets and martyrs who have gone against the crowd and surrendered the good will of their contemporaries because they have had in themselves an ideal to which they wished to be true. It is of the essence of such an ideal that it is absolute and universal; the lone prophet's act carries with it the implication of a standard which would be that, not of any temporary observer, but of the completely impartial and universal observer.

In addition to these strange desires there is another which is felt very generally, perhaps universally, the desire to feel at home in the world as a whole and to be in harmony with its deepest tendencies. In many this becomes a real desire to believe that there is at the heart of all things a Power which sustains us in our finest efforts and aids us in our allegiance to ideal ends. If we could believe that our search for beauty and worth and our sacrifice of temporary satisfaction for more enduring ones were rooted in the very nature of things and were carried on by One stronger than ourselves, human life would become radiant. No longer should we be strange creatures with curious desires, but our highest values would be conserved and increased by the Master of the universe. Our lives would not be alien events, but would be full of meaning.

There are many persons who not only desire the assurance that there is One at the heart of all things who cares for the values about which we care most at our best moments; they also report that they have had an experience of fellowship with Him. They have found an answer to their searchings, a response to their lonely cries. They have found a "presence in the midst," a companion that followed with them on life's darkest as well as life's brightest ways. This experience seems to them indubitably real, and, since real, the most important thing in their lives. And this One whom they believe they have *known* at first hand they call God. They believe many more things about Him, but the chief glory of their lives arises from the fact that they have *met* Him.

We are now in a better position to say what the churches mean and what religion is. Religion is at once the result of a desire and an experience. All desires and all experiences come within its scope sooner or later, but religion exists primarily because of the human desire to believe in a Sustainer of our ideals and the human experience of knowing that Sustainer.

The results of the union of this desire and this experience have been various, and monuments to this union are all over our globe. Men who have known the union of the desire and the experience have not been able to take it lightly, but have felt constrained to express their wonder in appropriate and worthy ways. They have built structures in which to meet by celebrating the tremendous fact, sometimes plain meetinghouses, sometimes ornate churches, sometimes rude altars in the open air. Usually they have been eager to produce houses which are better and more beautiful than other houses, and thus the desire for beauty comes into the service of the desire for God. It is not insignificant that so many of the ancient structures which have remained to this day are temples. Men might build poorly for themselves, but they felt constrained to build enduringly for the gods. The flair for poetry has likewise been drawn into service. Men have used language to make prayers and hymns that will express faithfully our deepest aspirations. Words have been used, but not mere words; there has been a demand that they should be the best words.

The desire to be worthy has likewise come into the service of the desire for God. Men have believed increasingly that they could express their wonder and gratitude, not only by noble structures, not only by fine words, but even more by courageous and splendid living. "And what," asked the Prophet, "doth the Lord require of thee, but to do justly, to love mercy, and to walk humbly with thy God?" When the church is at low ebb it may be hard to see any difference in the moral standards of those who go to the churches and those who do not, but it should also be seen that in many periods the church has been a moral pioneer. Even now, many of the moral persons who are away from the churches may be influenced by them when they little realize the ultimate source of the deepest influences upon them.

We may state the matter somewhat differently by saying that religion exists because of *rever-*

ence. This word epitomizes the meaning of religion better than any other single expression now in use. Two contemporary British authors have shown why this is.

For by reverence we mean a complex emotional attitude which manifests just this combination of abasement and exaltation, awe and confidence. That for which we feel reverence must go wholly beyond us and yet not be utterly alien to us. We feel, as we say, "small" but we also feel exalted by contact and kinship with the object of our veneration.[3]

Man is so made that he feels reverence for the Power in virtue of which nature harbors ideal ends. For many this Power is a Person with whom they believe they have communion, but the closeness of the communion does not overcome the reverence. The wonder is so great in the minds of all who grasp what religion is trying to say that, while they are religious, they can never descend to the trivial. The truly religious man is at home in his world, there is a ligament between him and the Heart of things, but the presence of the ligament does not keep him from being filled with awe. If a man really believed that he had been in the very presence of the Maker and Sustainer

[3] A. Barratt Brown and John W. Harvey, *The Naturalness of Religion.* London, 1929, p. 40.

of all that is, the Upholder of ideal ends, could he ever again fail to wonder? Would not his whole life be lifted to a plane of reverence so exalted that all ground would appear as holy ground?

The sense of reverence which arises from the union of a perennial desire with an indubitable experience has appeared in all peoples, but with varying results. Some religions have been ennobling and some have been degrading. Superstition, ignorance, cruelty, and military zeal have all been connected with religion and have changed it accordingly. Religions have a tendency to become external and lose their inner meaning, to become merely ceremonial and lose their moral vigor. Throughout human history it has been necessary, again and again, for lone prophets to come forward and warn their contemporaries against their failure to maintain the high ideal set before them. If it is religion that becomes debased it is also religion that produces the men who cleanse it and set the feet of men on new paths. Religion is often our curse, but it may always be our blessing.

For better or for worse we are religious men and we may as well accept the fact. We desire, we believe, we experience, we aspire, and the indications are that all this will continue. We need

13

not be frightened by those who speak continually of the dim barbaric origins of religion, suggesting by this means that it is ultimately reducible to ignorant and savage fear, and therefore something which the human spirit will outgrow. Religion, like anything else by which we live, did undoubtedly have low origins, but it is only by a curious logic that we *identify* anything with its origins. Our real interest is in what religion has developed *into*, not in what it came *from*.

We need nothing more than a clear statement of the genetic or historical method to see its grave limitations. This statement was made by a master hand a half century ago when the historical method was in its first flush of success:

> In the last century men asked of a belief or a story, Is it true? We now ask, How did men come to take it for true? In short the relations among social phenomena which now engage most attention, are relations of original source, rather than those of actual consistency in theory and actual fitness in practice. The devotees of the current method are more concerned with the pedigree and genealogical connection of a custom or an idea than with its own proper goodness or badness, its strength or its weakness.[4]

There are many splendid works which attempt to give the "pedigree and genealogical connection"

[4] John Morley, *On Compromise*. London, 1917, p. 31.

of religion, but such an inquiry is no part of the present work. If our minds can be freed from the subtle charm of geneticism we shall be able to see religion as a present fact, something to be understood and evaluated for what it is *now* rather than for what it *was* in its crude beginnings. But even those crude beginnings, rightly understood, already included an irreducible element. At even its lowest the religious experience is not the same as fear or as reaction to the strange. It is the great merit of Professor Otto's famous book that he has clarified this point.[5] He has shown that "the Holy" is not the same as anything else, that it is genuinely *sui generis*.

Religion is not something that can be explained away, but must be faced as a unique and important human experience. It is not the same as philosophy, because while philosophy is a matter of intellectual and critical inquiry, with all that is, as the object of the inquiry, religion is a matter of the total response of the self to a particular aspect of the whole. Philosophy may well include religion in its purview and may lead to a position of belief in God, but it does not *become* religion. The point is well made by Archbishop Temple in

[5] Cf. Rudolph Otto, *Das Heilige;* translation by John W. Harvey, as *The Idea of the Holy.* London, 1923.

his Gifford Lectures: "The heart of Religion is not an opinion about God, such as Philosophy might reach as the conclusion of its argument; it is a personal relationship with God."[6]

At the same time religion is by no means identical with science, though the man of science usually gives evidence of a strong religion, either consciously or unconsciously experienced. When a man classifies and measures phenomena and draws general conclusions regarding their behavior, he is a scientist, but when the same man views the scene before him with reverence he has entered another realm. "It is the result of no little culture," wrote Matthew Arnold, "to attain to a clear perception that science and religion are two wholly different things." We may all be comforted, as Arnold was, by the thought that "while the multitude imagines itself to live by its false science, it does really live by its true religion."[7]

The one aspect of life to which religion is most akin is poetry and especially love poetry. We cannot go as far as Arnold did in identifying religion and poetry,[8] for that, again, would be to deny religion's irreducible character, but the kin-

[6] William Temple, *Nature, Man and God.* London, 1934, p. 54.
[7] Matthew Arnold, *Essays in Criticism,* First Series. London, 1902, pp. 28, 29.
[8] *Ibid.,* Second Series, 1900, pp. 1 *ff.*

ship is instructive. The poet goes beyond facts to meanings; he sees the world, not as something to be measured or even analyzed, but as something to which his whole being must respond. He catches a glimpse of what the world is like beneath its outer husks and what he sees makes him sing. Perhaps the kinship is best explained by the assumption that the genuine poet is, like other men, incurably religious, and is different only because he has a unique gift of penetration or expression or both.

Man cannot live by bread alone, and he cannot live by prose alone. He goes about his practical tasks which keep up the mechanics of living, but these never suffice. The dull prose fails to satisfy and men of all ages break forth into praise and song and prayer which bake no bread. Old temples lose their hold on the imagination, but new temples are built to take their places. Sometimes they are better than the old ones; sometimes they are worse; but the building goes on. It is amazing that men ever discovered the use of fire, but it is far more amazing that, once fire was discovered, it was used to kindle a flame at an altar.

II. Spiritual Religion and Belief

In the previous chapter it was pointed out that religion rests upon both a deep-seated desire and an indubitable experience. When we come to examine the structure raised on these foundations we realize soon that it is somehow a matter of belief. A man's religion is often referred to as his *creed* and statements of belief occupy a large part in many public celebrations of religion. We need to ask what part belief actually plays in the religion of most men and what part it *should* play.

In the first place, it must be made abundantly clear that belief is important. What an individual really believes about the nature of the world, the character of God, and the possibilities of man will be sure to affect his practical conduct in many far-reaching ways. A man's general world view is the most significant thing about him because it determines the details of his life. If a man gives his time sacrificially, it is because he has a conception of life which includes self-sacrifice as a valid ideal. What we are doing *in toto*, in other words, determines what we do piecemeal, and a creed is really an attempt to say what we are doing *in toto*.

We constantly make our practical decisions by reference to our larger convictions. If we are in some doubt concerning the profession we should enter we solve the problem, if we are intelligent, not by doing the thing that is easiest and nearest at hand, but by trying to determine which profession is most likely to contribute to those ends about which we really care. A statement about the things for which we really care would be a creed, a formulation of ultimate belief. The completely selfish man, if such there be, does as he does because he really believes that the most important thing in life is personal advancement.

Matthew Arnold said that conduct was three-fourths of life. It would be more true to say that belief occupies that relative position, because belief includes within it so many of the springs of conduct. Consider, for example, what a genuine belief in Jesus Christ would entail. A person who was wholly convinced that the life of Jesus was a veritable revelation of the eternal Father would

surely bend every effort to be like Jesus in word
and deed. Our belief might be belief in man. Let
us say that we believe in a core of decency in each
human being, in spite of many appearances to the
contrary. That belief, rightly understood, may
carry with it a host of consequences such as the
release from racial animosity and from the national hatred which participation in war entails.
Let us say a man really believes in God as his
Creator and Sustainer. The whole mood of his
life will be different from what it would be if he
only believed in the human conscience and elected
to call that God. If we are trying to understand
a person, it is highly important to know, not only
whether he believes in God, but also what he
believes about God.

We must not so stress belief, however, as to
suggest that the roots of conduct are primarily or
solely intellectual. We are often tempted to cham-
pion the Socratic view that all evildoing is the
result of ignorance, that if a man really knew
better he would do better, but the mass of evidence concerning the inner life is to the contrary.
In all generations men, and particularly Christian
men, have admitted that they have gone deliberately against the highest they have known.
Belief is important, but belief alone will not suf-

fice and, though a man cannot do *without* a creed, he cannot do with *only* a creed.

Important as belief is, it can easily be overstressed. It has sometimes been stressed in such a way as to be prejudicial to the interests of spiritual religion. Men have set up creeds as barriers between themselves and other men and have refused to have religious fellowship with any who could not subscribe to the items in a given declaration. The weeding out of heretics has been a common enterprise for centuries and goes on today, though usually in more subtle ways than before. The tragedy is that faith is always enfeebled whenever it is expressed in a static form of words; something valuable is always lost. The hard form of the words cannot give the central spirit of religion and thus many of the most spiritually alert persons are alienated. It surely is no accident that the prophets who are honored in succeeding generations have so often been looked upon as heretics in their own time. A creed is, from its very nature, static and hard and a poor receptacle for the pulsating life of the spirit.

The person who refuses to be bound by some given creed may be one who cannot accept the declaration in question because of a larger faith of his own which rules out what he considers a smaller one. Leslie Stephen did good service, when our fathers were young, by pointing out, in *An Agnostic's Apology*, that he was actuated by a faith in the dependability of nature. This was to him so central that he had to eliminate from the creeds all that opposed it. Stephen's belief made impossible for him a belief in miracles in the usual sense. It was not that he had any objection to miracles, but he did have a larger creed which entailed their denial.[1] It ought to be recognized, then, that the unbeliever, in any particular instance, may be in reality a person of great beliefs of his own by which he is willing to live.

The upholder of a spiritual religion is really faced, therefore, with a difficult dilemma when he is asked what he believes. If we try to make a compact statement, whether affirmative or negative, we always have the feeling that the heart of the matter has escaped us, for spiritual religion cannot be reduced to a few neat phrases. The five or six affirmations or denials seem to have almost no relation to the elevating experience that has driven men to build altars in all generations. The result is that we give husks when the honest

---

[1] Cf. Leslie Stephen, *An Agnostic's Apology*, Second Edition. New York, 1903. For stress on the thought that all creeds have negative as well as positive aspects, see p. 49.

seeker has asked for bread. The honest seeker really wants to understand the secret springs by which religious men live, and instead we give a theological formula. Perhaps, for this reason, we ought not to try to explain. Perhaps we ought to say: "Live among us, worship with us; attempt to become a sharer in the corporate life of the religious group. Then the question will be already answered. Then you will know what we believe because you will see what we live by."

The other horn of the dilemma is no more satisfactory, though many of the liberal persuasion are driven to it. The usual alternative to a statement of belief lies in saying that spiritual religion is *free*, that it has no belief. "It makes no difference what you believe," we say; "you may believe as you like and yet be religious in a truly spiritual sense." This alternative seems to accord with the fact presented by our great variety, but consider the effect on the sincere questioner. He has been searching for the secret of spiritual life, but we do not satisfy him. When he asks for bread we give him not even a creedal husk; we offer him nothing at all.

The first horn of our creedal dilemma seems to involve us in dogmatic narrowness, where the life of the spirit is squeezed out; but the second

23

horn involves us in arid liberalism, where belief has ceased to matter. We are then only a step away from the luncheon clubs of the cheaper variety where fellowship is *mere* fellowship. When we consider the matter carefully, none of us is willing to accept either horn of the dilemma. We are not willing to limit our faith to a barren intellectual formula, on the one hand, nor to overlook faith entirely in extreme emphasis on mere good works, on the other. We see the dangers of dogmatism and we also see the dangers of an easy tolerance which is little more than indifference. How shall we make an answer, when questioned, which shall say neither too much nor too little?

We are on solid ground when we show that a truly spiritual religion necessitates sound belief on cardinal points, but likewise necessitates a loving spirit. Religion without the former can degenerate into sentimentality, while religion without the latter becomes hard and censorious. The essence of our religious position will be understood by other people, not merely by what we say, but also by the manner in which we say it.

The attitude of spiritual religion in the matter of belief may be conveniently summarized by saying that it stands for "critical tolerance." The adjective is needed because tolerance, without

safeguards, can become a doubtful virtue. Tolerance may be nothing more than the easy acquies-
cence of a person who does not wish to be
disturbed because he doesn't really *care*. Tolerance has appeared in the past chiefly among those
who accept the received order with little worry
or thought, and the merely tolerant person is seldom a world shaker.

We often suppose that intolerance is found
almost wholly among conservatives, but a moment's thought will show that this is not the case.
Advanced thinkers, who take their thought seriously, are apt to be acutely intolerant. They
may want freedom to think as they please, but
they are often unwilling to permit such freedom
on the part of others, because they think the
others are *wrong* in their thought. The Puritan
experience in Colonial Boston is a case in point.

In some rare instances, on the part of individuals and groups, there has appeared a combination of advanced thought and a willingness to
allow others to think differently, even though
erroneously. This has arisen, not from a failure
to care, but from a lively conviction that the
world is great, the ways of God mysterious, and
the leadings of the Spirit wonderfully diverse.
These upholders of critical tolerance have said

25

in substance to their fellows: "We think you have arrived at wrong conclusions, but we recognize that you are following the truth as you see it, just as we are following the truth as we see it, and we therefore hope you will uphold your conclusions faithfully. We hope that while you uphold your position you may ever be open to new light as it may break forth in God's world and that we may be equally open to it." The apostles of this kind of tolerance, says Professor Whitehead, "should be commemorated in every laboratory, in every church, and in every court of law."[2]

We see, then, the place that belief must hold in a genuinely spiritual religion. Belief will be important, but it will be understood that any particular creed is only an outer shell and can never do justice to the inner kernel of religious life. This, indeed, was the great message of Thomas Carlyle when he wrote *Sartor Resartus* over a century ago.[3] Carlyle knew the value of belief, but he

[2] Alfred North Whitehead, *Adventures of Ideas*. New York, 1933, p. 63.

[3] Carlyle has helped many men to achieve their first understanding of the difference between religion and theology. His expression is so unrestrained that he cannot be followed as a guide in careful thought, and he often loses his way in a burst of rhetoric, but he is still valuable as one who stimulates in men the hope that there *can be* a spiritual religion. In any case, he makes his reader conscious of the difference between the clothing and that which is clothed.

knew also how easy it is to confuse the outer vest-
ments, the work of the tailor, with the inner fact.
We must not make the mistake so often made, of
despising theology, but we must recognize clearly
its essential limitations. Scientific theology as the
reasoned account of religious convictions is necessary, but the account must never be confused with
that for which we account. Religion is like falling
in love; theology is like a treatise on courtship.
Religion is fairly constant, so constant, indeed,
that John Greenleaf Whittier and the author of
the Book of Job are spiritual brothers, but theology, like any science, tends to change greatly from
age to age. "Religion," writes Dean Sperry with
fine precision, "is the initial fact, theology is the
reflective science which attempts to interpret the
fact."[4]

We must make and remake our creeds, but we
must hold to them with a certain spiritual modesty
and humility, modesty and humility arising from
a sense of the contrast between the greatness of
God and the smallness of our powers of understanding. Our deepest religious convictions must
be stated, refined, and defended, but they must
always be tempered with love. We seek a critical

[4] Willard L. Sperry, *What You Owe Your Child.* New York,
1935, p. 36.

27

tolerance which arises *along with* strong conviction, not *in place of* strong conviction. We need great believers who are loving and great lovers of mankind who really believe. In the following chapters there will be presented the outlines of a world view and life view which is really the creed of a number of persons. But these affirmations are presented with humility and respect, humility because the world is always greater than our understanding of it, and respect because good men have arrived at different conclusions. The positions outlined are held firmly, but it is also hoped that they are held with tenderness of spirit. The motto of this chapter might be "not less but more," not less belief, but more love.

III. The Spiritual Inwardness of Jesus

Though religion is universal, it appears characteristically in the form of some particular and historical faith. Few men have religion *as* religion; they share in some particular religious tradition and profit by the accumulated thoughts and practices of countless men who have preceded them. Of these particular embodiments of religion the most important, at least for Western man, is Christianity.

Christianity is a complex, composite product of mystery cults, prophetic Judaism, philosophic Hellenism, practical Romanism, and militant Teutonism, but all the diverse parts are held together by a powerful link—the person of Jesus. Jesus was, so far as appearance went, a humble artisan of northern Palestine who lived in the time of Rome's greatness and lived in such a way that his words, deeds, and death were cherished by increasing numbers as sacred memories. About a half century after his death, accounts of his words and deeds were written out, depending manifestly, however, on earlier records of the same. The character presented in these brief biographies has appealed to numberless men and women as the most beautiful thing in the world, and lives have been greatly influenced by mere acquaintance with the portrait that has been preserved. We make the birth of this person our historical date line.

The almost universal esteem in which the memory of Jesus Christ is held is one of the most amazing facts of history and one of the most encouraging. This universality of esteem tells us a great deal, not only about Jesus, but about mankind in general, for people can be understood, in large part, in terms of their admirations. As Emerson stated the matter, "We can only see what we are."[1] The very ability to appreciate art is indicative of an element of artistic genius, and the same would seem to be true of character as well.

We see so much misplaced admiration in the world that the almost universal recognition of Christ is the more surprising. Why should the

[1] Ralph Waldo Emerson, *Conduct of Life*. Boston, 1888, p. 221.

30

highest admiration be so well placed when lesser admirations are so poorly placed? How strange, in view of our perennial war fever, that the universal focus of admiration has not been upon the conventional strong man, the man on horseback! Yet the sober truth is that millions have spoken in hushed tones of a person who not only had no army, but actually rebuked a follower for using a sword in the Master's defense. All this is almost too good to be true and we almost pinch ourselves to prove that we are not dreaming. Perhaps the common man can be trusted when it comes to the genuinely great, even though he cannot be so trusted in lesser things. It is heartening, for example, to consider the general appreciation for a really noble poem like Gray's *Elegy*.[2]

What was the character of this person who has so caught the imagination of millions that many of them have believed him more than human? Most of his life was spent in common toil, but, at about the age of thirty, he entered upon a brief public career which was made up of teaching in various villages, private instruction to a

[2] The popularity of the poem was not completely pleasing to the poet because he thought the popularity derived from the subject rather than from his treatment of it. Experience has shown that this fear was unjustified since other poems have dealt with similar subjects. Of course the interest in the subject itself is highly instructive to the student of human nature.

31

few intimate followers, and remarkable deeds, especially healings, both mental and physical. His career came swiftly to an end with the infliction of the death penalty, ostensibly for political reasons. Later his intimate followers became convinced that he had somehow proved to be superior to death and that his career, instead of being limited to a few months, was an eternal one.

As we examine the teaching which has been so beautifully preserved for us, and look for unity in it, we find that unity in the note of spiritual inwardness. We have, happily, passed the time when it was almost conventional to present Jesus as a political and social reformer or perhaps the founder of socialism. That he did have aspects of his message that were and are capable of extremely important social application is certainly true, and some such applications will be mentioned in the sequel, but it is surely a great mistake to make Jesus merely a glorified reformer. We can do so only by deliberately ignoring much of the recorded teaching.

One of the most valuable tendencies in modern Gospel scholarship is that which emphasizes the apocalyptic aspect of the message of Jesus. If we take seriously entire blocks of the extant Gospels we must suppose that Jesus shared the expectation of a sudden change in the world order, a change to be made by God rather than by men, though men might be factors in it in virtue of their willingness or unwillingness to fulfill certain conditions. But our danger now is that we shall go to an extreme in the apocalyptic interpretation of Jesus, and this is no better than an extreme emphasis in the direction of the social gospel. As a matter of fact, there are elements in the teaching of Jesus which no candid person can minimize, that are hard to harmonize with an apocalyptic world view. For one thing, the apocalyptic theory of history is fundamentally pessimistic, at least so far as this world is concerned, and the absolute trust in God the Father, without whom not a sparrow falls, is fundamentally optimistic, regarding *this* world or any other, for though we change rooms we cannot go out from under the Father's roof. It is a profound saying that "there are many rooms in my Father's house," and the point of this profound saying is lost only because the familiar word "mansions" carries with it such a freight of irreligious associations.[3]

[3] The reader who desires a brief and competent treatment of the question of the apocalyptic element in the teaching of Jesus cannot do better than to read E. F. Scott, *The Ethical Teaching of Jesus*. New York, 1924.

33

If Jesus did hope for social changes, his hope was shot through with the spiritual inwardness of his message so that it was men's hearts as well as systems that needed change, and if his theory of history was partly apocalyptic, then for once at least this theory was completely spiritualized. In any case, Jesus preached absolute trust in a sovereign God who is reigning now. God was to him absolutely real, genuinely careful of each lone individual in the world, and absolutely loving as well as just. Religion consists in worshiping God and being like Him, that is, completely and powerfully loving. Religion has a constant tendency to degenerate into an emphasis on externals, but Jesus, like the Hebrew prophets before Him, pointed continually to the prime necessity of an inner spirit.

A religion of spiritual inwardness, such as Jesus taught, must fight on at least three fronts to maintain its integrity. In the first place, it must fight against *ceremonialism*. Religion has always had ceremonial features, it has always involved a cult, but that is not the same as saying that religion *is* a cult. It is easy to show that powerful religious leaders and thinkers of all times have been at great pains to distinguish between the essential religion and its ceremonial manifestation. About religion there is always lingering some vestigial magic, so that men are prone to suppose the correct performance of acts and gestures will suffice. Sometimes, as in Judaism, the danger lies in emphasis on animal sacrifice, sometimes it lies in stress on liturgical form, sometimes on church attendance. The arguments concerning the amount of water to be used in baptism, the words to be used during baptism, and the place in which the ceremony should be performed are both tragic and comic.

Ceremonial acts, such as kneeling and bowing, the observance of special days, the institution of fasts—all these may *help* the spirit of man as he seeks God, but we must go beyond them. Jesus, as his words indicate, was afraid men would be satisfied with the husk instead of going on to find the living kernel within. It is all very well, he suggests, to tithe mint and rue and all manner of herbs, *unless,* as a result, you "pass over judgment and the love of God."

In the second place, a religion of spiritual inwardness, such as Jesus taught, must be on guard against *creedalism*. Creeds are extremely important, as was indicated in the foregoing chapter of this book, but it has been easy to make a creed an external thing, so that a man could have theological correctness without a loving heart. Jesus knew and said, as the prophets had said before him, how easy it is for men to honor God with their lips while their hearts are far from Him. An intellectual formulation of faith, fine as it may be and necessary as it may be, is external, and it is the inner life that counts. There is a world of difference between a *discussion of God* in a classroom and *God* as the prime reality of a man's life.

In the third place, Jesus, in teaching a religion of spiritual inwardness, had to oppose *ethical legalism*. He knew very well that a man may have outer moral correctness, just as he may have creedal and ceremonial correctness, and yet be a thoroughly detestable person. It is possible to keep the Ten Commandments and yet not be a Christian. A great many of the reported sayings of Jesus show that he had in mind the Jewish law, a thing sacred to him, and that he wanted it to occupy the proper place in life. The follower of Jesus respects the law, but he goes beyond it; he stresses the inner spirit from which right acts must come. Jesus goes beyond murder to hatred, beyond adultery to lust, beyond alms to love. He laid down not laws, but principles for the guidance of the inner life, principles clarified by

36

the use of illustrations which we call parables. His teaching is not hedged about by qualifying phrases, as is a legal code; he gives the idea, and we must make the application. What Jesus demands is a new will; he leads men to the adoption of an ethical mysticism. We must not suppose that Jesus opposed the externals of religious faith. The externals we shall always have, for even an absence of form becomes a new form, but Jesus teaches that the outer must not be allowed to obscure the inner aspect of religion. His principle is that of "not less but more." This ye ought to have done, and not to have left the other undone.

It is one of the most striking ironies of all history that the very religion of which Jesus was the founder should present continual examples of what he opposed. After his clear teaching regarding the proper place of ceremonial, men, acting in his name, have denied fellowship to those who have not experienced certain rites, which supposedly have the authority of Jesus' words behind them. In the same way doctrinal correctness regarding the nature of Jesus has frequently been more emphasized than any other single item in the entire Christian system. The result is that many have mouthed his name and yet have not caught at all the infection of his spirit. After so much teaching regarding the dangers of ethical legalism, the very statements of Jesus have frequently been regarded as external rules which must be obeyed to the letter. But this irony only shows that the message of spiritual inwardness is one that is needed anew in every generation.

It is probably true that there is something of value in all world religions, but this is not tantamount to the assertion that all religions are of equal value. It is probably true that great insights have come regarding the spiritual life in all generations, but this does not involve the further conclusion that all insights are of equal merit. It is thoroughly possible that one religion is far superior to others and that the spiritual insights of one person are incomparably more important than the spiritual insights of others. It is the conviction of a great many careful thinkers that Christianity, so long as it is true to its original foundation, is far superior to any other religion that the world has known and that the character of Jesus is a unique fact in the world. These conclusions have been affirmed by the millions who have believed in what is called the Christian revelation and have held that Jesus was divine.

Our generation is much in danger of an over-dose of relativism. Some little knowledge of comparative religions and of comparative ethical standards has had a subtle and sometimes unwholesome influence, leading us to the immature conclusion that one thing is just as good as another. It is possible, however, to make a cogent defense of absolutism either in morals or in religion. There may be an absolute standard from which the others deviate to their detriment.[4]

The normal human being, when he is carefully presented with the portrait of Jesus as found in the Gospels, is drawn irresistibly to the person there depicted, and the conclusion regarding the uniqueness of Jesus in history comes as a *result* of experience, rather than as a prior form into which experience is made to fit. If we call him "Lord" because it is customary to do so, we may be very far from his spirit, but if our words come

---

[4] The thoughtful reader who cares to consider the argument for ethical absolutism should consult the really remarkable treatise of Nikolai Hartmann. The English translation, called *Ethics*, was published in 1932. For the thesis that Christianity is the absolute religion, see Adolf Harnack, *What is Christianity?* (London, 1904, p. 65 *ff.*) For a somewhat different statement of the thesis, see Bishop Westcott, *Essays in the History of Religious Thought in the West* (London, 1891). A more modern and less extreme form of the religious argument is that of Dr. Albert Schweitzer in *Christianity and the Religions of the World* (London, 1923).

out of a great inner experience we are indeed his disciples.

It was the message of Christ that true religion consists in a pure and loving inner spring of thought and action, and it is the experience of men that this inner life is best nourished as we hold always before our vision the fact of the one who has thus taught us. Jesus is, and should be, not only Master, but Lord as well. In the light of the reality of direct experience the familiar distinction between the religion of Jesus and the religion *about* Jesus is transcended. As we bow before him we are better able to follow his teaching. Religion is more than incense or pilgrimages or sacred words; true religion consists in the love of God, and we love God better when we know Jesus more. Jesus, therefore, was not merely the Teacher who announced the principles of spiritual religion; he was also the Lord and Master, in loyalty to whom spiritual religion becomes a reality.

IV. The Spiritual Nature of God

From earliest times men have believed in some "higher powers," but often the conception of them has been crude and crass. Religion in its earliest stages is closely tied up with magic, so that the religious man is one who attempts to subject the higher powers to his own coercive control. Religion at the magical level, a level not completely overcome,[1] is the manipulation of both friendly and unfriendly powers in the interests of human success. The gods are powerful, but they can be flattered or tricked or made to stand and deliver, providing the proper rites, incantations, and ceremonial formulæ are employed. The prayer is efficacious, providing it includes the correct phrases. Even in our own time there are many who feel unhappy about a prayer and doubtful of its value

---

[1] Witness the regular practice of many motorists who seek a priest's blessing on their motor cars.

THE ESSENCE OF SPIRITUAL RELIGION

if it does not end with the familiar words, "and this we ask in Jesus' name."

The god of magic, whether the magic be that of a primitive "medicine man" or of a twentieth-century Western man, is unworthy of our worship and love. Since he can be manipulated he is really inferior, and since he can be flattered he is really ignoble. Much skepticism in our day rests upon this prespiritual and debasing conception of God, for it is a conception which carries with it the seeds of its own destruction. As men become more intelligent they are bound to discover that the formulæ are not efficacious and, if this is the only idea of God they have had, they are bound to conclude that experience of fellowship with God is nothing but an illusion.

In the same way the thought of God as a material or physical entity is bound for self-destruction. If the gods are really supposed to be physical creatures living on Mount Olympus, the time will come when some courageous man will climb the mountain, and when he climbs he will find no such gods as have been described. If the gods are physical they must, sooner or later, be apprehended by the senses, and primitive skepticism begins when the observation is made by intelligent men that the gods are not so apprehended. The gods are never seen with the eyes, unless the individual has an hallucination, and men early understood the possibility of self-delusion in sensory matters. The wrought-up individual may "hear" physical voices, but a religion which rested its case on an experience so manifestly subjective would not long be able to command the attention of either intelligent or honest persons.

Just as it is dangerous to talk seriously about the gods on Olympus, so is it equally dangerous to talk about heaven as a place. The modern counterpart of the Olympic climber is the astronomer who scans the universe and finds no physical abode of the blessed. A few might be able to overlook this negative evidence, but the majority cannot, and a religion which localizes or materializes the divine produces ultimately its own defeat.

Considerations like the above have driven thoughtful and devout men to adopt a conception of God as thoroughly spiritual. The most important pronouncement in this whole movement for the spiritualization of the idea of God is found in the words of Jesus to the woman of Samaria at Jacob's well: *"God is a Spirit: and they that worship him must worship him in spirit and in truth."* The nobler souls in religion had

43

long been approaching this position before the time of Jesus and the nobler souls since have tried to appropriate it, though it is probable that vestiges of the magical and materialistic view always remain with us in spite of our determination to pass beyond them.

What do we mean by saying God is Spirit? We mean, in the first place, that He differs from the material world in somewhat the same manner that we differ from our bodies. We shall consider carefully in the next chapter what we mean by spirit in mankind, but here it may be said in passing that no man is a practicing materialist. Men talk of materialism in philosophical dialogues, but it may be safely asserted that no man feels like a materialist. Our common language of everyday life betrays the distinction we make between ourselves and our bodies which we *use*. The arguments for materialism are old and well known and can be reduced without violence to the known fact that we are *affected by* the physical state of our bodies. The logical status of this proposition is not the same as that of the further proposition that we are *nothing but* our bodies. For centuries it has been known that behavior is changed by the use of drugs and that a man may forget or have foolish ideas if he is struck on the head. These

44

well-known facts suggest that we are *conditioned by* material things, but it does not follow that we are to be *reduced to* material things.

As a matter of fact we are far better acquainted with spirit than with matter. We are mere on-lookers when we note how one physical event causes another physical event, but we are partici-pators when we *produce* a physical event or an-other mental event. Matter we must always ob-serve from the outside, but we know spirit from the inside. We may not be able to know spirit by description, but that is unnecessary; we know it by acquaintance.

The man who believes in the spiritual nature of God is interpreting the world in terms of what he knows best. He is saying that the deepest reality about the world is a Principle, Power, or Person who differs from matter as we differ from matter. We go on, however, to make a significant addition in holding that, while we are conditioned by localized bodies in space, God is not so con-ditioned and limited. To believe in God in the spiritual sense is to believe in a Spirit as real as ourselves, but not limited as we are limited. It is obvious, then, that He is not to be worshiped in one place rather than another, as Jesus told the Samaritan woman, and that He is not to be addressed by any particular tongue or reached by any particular formula. The holiest experience we know between two finite spirits is that of love or friendship, in which there is unity without a denial of distinctness, and this, at its highest, is relatively independent of physical contact or even words. If God is Spirit, we may suppose that the love of God is like love between finite spirits, but freed from its limitations.

It is important to observe that Jesus, as well as most of his followers, believed, in addition, that the God who is Spirit is also completely loving and completely providential. He wants the welfare of each individual soul and He cares for each one with infinite patience. This is an essentially simple and childlike faith, one looked upon with disdain by many sophisticates, but it is doubtful if a fully developed spiritual religion can avoid it. If we deny the reality of providence we have so removed God from intimate control over our lives that religion ceases, in any vital sense. This was seen and ably expressed long ago by Cicero in his famous treatise on the *Nature of the Gods*. "For there are and have been," he says, "philosophers who hold that the gods exercise no control over human affairs whatever. But if their opinion is the true one, how can piety, reverence or religion

46

exist?"[1] If piety goes, religion goes, and piety rests on the childlike faith in the continual loving presence of God in our minutest affairs.

The chief objection, of course, to a belief in providence is a recognition of the problem of evil. This problem arises for believers when they admit the fact of undeserved suffering in the world. No man knows a complete answer to this problem, though the genuinely religious man has usually been satisfied with the answer implied in the Book of Job to the effect that we are too small to understand, and God is working at something bigger than we can appreciate. Perhaps in the religious man's belief in providence and his amazement at the fact of unmerited suffering we have an antinomy of the spiritual life as real as the metaphysical antinomies presented by Kant. We cannot let go our belief, on the one hand, that the very hairs of our heads are numbered, and, on the other hand, we cannot let go our belief in a morally intelligible economy of nature. It is the conviction of developed spiritual religion that two such necessary positions are not ultimately incompatible. The working solution of Job or anyone else is that of trust.

[1] Cicero, *De Natura Deorum*, I, ii, Loeb Classical Library; translation by H. Rackham.

47

It is not surprising that Jesus so often refers to a little child as a pattern to be followed. Spiritual religion starts, as a little child does, with wonder and trust, and no one can enter the gates of its domain who does not enter in that mood. We have to begin our world picture with some initial premise, and we begin ours with the primitive proposition that this is God's world, every bit of it. God is an infinite Spirit, completely loving, and our lives are in His hands. He is the deepest reality of our lives, far more real and important than are sticks and stones. When we do not see His loving hand in all things, it is because we are too small to understand or because our vision is dimmed by selfishness. Probably no prose writer has ever stated this attitude of complete trust better than did Addison, though we do not consider him a religious writer.

He sees at one view the whole thread of my existence, not only that part of it which I have already passed through, but that which runs forward into all the depths of eternity. When I lay me down to sleep, I recommend myself to his care; when I awake, I give myself up to his direction. Amidst all the evils that threaten me, I will look up to him for help, and question not but he will either avert them, or turn them to my advantage. Though I know neither the time nor the manner of the death I am to die, I am not at all solicitous about it, because I am sure that he knows them both, and that he will not fail to comfort and support me under them.[3]

It is really something of a tragedy that certain lines of Whittier's profoundly religious poetry should have become so very well known. We know them so well now that they are almost banal, and we miss the remarkable beauty of the view they present. Whittier is the poet of simplehearted, childlike, spiritual religion, and it is instructive to note the growing popularity of his poems that have been set to music. They are sung all over the world. In his not too well-known poem called "Trust," Whittier states accurately the position which is defended in this chapter. The poem begins:

> The same old baffling questions! O my friend,
> I cannot answer them.

and ends as follows:

> I have no answer for myself or thee,
> Save that I learned beside my mother's knee;
> "All is of God that is, and is to be;
> And God is good." Let this suffice us still,
> Resting in childlike trust upon His will
> Who moves to His great ends unthwarted by the ill.

Can such a conception of the world be true? It is

[3] Joseph Addison, Essay on "Omens," *Addison's Essays,* Golden Treasury Series. London, 1898, p. 325.

obvious that the answer cannot rest on any middle ground. Whittier's poem is either sublimely beautiful and true to fact, or it is revolting. To many it is the latter and they are sure the ideas thus expressed are unworthy of the attention of adult, realistic, scientific men. But to thousands of others it is the beginning truth, in terms of which other aspects of life and the world are to be understood.

Is it true? This is not the place to reconsider the old scholastic arguments for God. It is doubtful if they ever appeal greatly to any except those who are already convinced. The argument for God follows three general lines, with different great books stressing different lines of approach. These are: first, the argument from the world of nature, which is not understandable alone and needs further explanation in terms of supernature; second, the argument from man's moral nature; third, the argument from religious experience. The second and third together are much more persuasive than the first, but the argument gains by the cumulative force of all three approaches.

All aspects of life, as we know them, are incomplete in themselves and seem to cry out for something outside to complete the picture. This is most true of man's soul. Man exhibits longings which the world of nature cannot satisfy and which, we are constrained to suppose, are indicative of an extranatural origin. If we are not in a foolish bondage to mere size, we see nothing illogical in the supposition that the moral and spiritual life of this tiny creature of earth may be the most significant fact in the universe. Man *seems* at least to be a citizen of two worlds, one natural and one supernatural, and, for many thoughtful persons, the reality of God is the most obvious explanation of this phenomenon.[4]

The skeptic has his own answers to all the familiar arguments for God and these can be found in many books. The fact, however, that is the most effective in the minds of many is the fact that Jesus believed. It is thoroughly clear that Jesus' faith in God and God's continual providence was unlimited. If we have come to feel that in the character of Jesus we have met with something finer than we have ever known in any other part of the world's history, something genuinely unique, we cannot but be assured that we differ from him at our peril. When a problem is beyond

[4] I know personally of no single brief treatment of the problem of the validity of belief in God as good as that published by Professor A. E. Taylor in *Essays Catholic and Critical*, edited by E. G. Selwyn (New York, 1926). Professor Taylor's luminous essay is "The Vindication of Religion."

51

scientific verification, as this problem is, the insights of superior souls may be our most important criteria. Not all superior souls have believed in God who is Spirit, but even a partial list of those who have so believed is sobering.

The presence of the completely spiritual and loving God as the deepest fact of our lives, a presence which to many is a fact of experience, can neither be proved nor disproved by an appeal to the senses or an appeal to reason. The reality of God who is Spirit is neither a necessary conclusion nor an impossible conclusion. It belongs for all men to the realm of the possible, but it belongs, for some men, to the realm of the actual.

V. The Spiritual Nature of Man

One of the most enduring factors in civilization is man's interest in his own nature. Men have tried in all generations to know themselves and have been united by the nature of the problem rather than by the character of the conclusions reached. Man has long been called the reasoning animal, the laughing animal, the praying animal, and so on almost without end. More recently he has been called the metaphysical animal and the epistemological animal, but at least one fact becomes clear: whatever else man is, he is the "anthropological animal," the creature who is interested in himself.

The very nature of the problem, therefore, guides us to its answer. Man is distinguished from all other creatures on the earth by his self-consciousness, by the fact that he is concerned, not merely about things and outer events, but also about his own inner processes. Other creatures are obviously conscious of objects which they use in satisfying their needs and of the parts of their own bodies, but we have no evidence whatever that any creature other than man sets off his own self as a center of reference, distinguished from the not-self, that is, the rest of the world.

The idea that man is distinguished by self-consciousness is an old idea in the world, but we are only beginning to see the wealth of the implications involved. Indeed, it is only because man is conscious of himself that he has a world at all. If man did not have the idea of internality he could not have the idea of externality, and the probability is that the mere animal has no conception of objects as existing independently; things have meaning for the animal only when they tie in with his needs. Because man can cut the world apart into inner and outer, he has the materials which make possible the picture of the world as an ordered whole.

Another striking aspect of self-consciousness is that which relates to moral life. As we examine our own desires we discover that, though we want to be possessors of goods, we want more; we want to be the objects of attributes. We want money, it may be, but there are some things we refuse to do for any amount of money. We refuse the money, not merely because we want to have the good opinion of another; we refuse the money because we want the good opinion of ourselves. There are many things which most of us would never do, even if we were sure of being completely alone and ultimately undiscovered. This well-known fact helps us to realize something of the vast importance of the fact that man is the creature who looks within as well as without.

When we say that man is distinguished by his appreciation of and interest in his inner life we are saying, in essence, what religious men of all ages have said when they declared that man is distinguished by *spirit*, by *Geist*. When we are conscious of self we are already in the realm of spirit, we have gone beyond the confines of time and space and we are observing that from which the realms of time and space are observed. Matter is *inert*, vegetables are *alive*, animals are *conscious*, and man is *self-conscious*. The four levels of the world, then, with which we are familiar are (1) *matter*, (2) *life*, (3) *mind*, and (4) *spirit*. Man *has* a body, but he *is* a spirit.

When we have come this far we can see the reasons for man's partial uniqueness in other ways. He is not the only creature with a language, but he is the only creature with a language which transcends time and space, especially in its written form. Our language is concerned, not primarily with the spread of information to be used in practical tasks, but with the transfer of meaning from one spirit to another. Man is not the only creature who reasons, but he is apparently the only creature who reasons about his own inner life, and the major part of our reasoning is so directed. Man is probably not unique in that he dreams, but it is probable that he is unique in the kind of dreaming he does; his dreams include ideals which he uses to test and criticize his own inner life. It is not surprising that a self-conscious creature would also be an ideal-forming creature. As man observes himself, he is dissatisfied with what he finds and his ideal is the standard of *his dissatisfaction*. Finally, it is not surprising that man, and man alone, has developed a religion, that he has been truly described as the only creature who prays. Only a creature interested in the realities of the inner life could come to the notion of a source and foundation of that life, and one who has started with the desire for approbation will be driven on to the desire for the approbation of the "Ideal Spectator." Religion is based on the recognition that the Ideal Spectator is more than an idea and is indeed the basic reality of the world.

If we are agreed, then, that God, as Jesus taught, is Spirit, and that man is spirit, the old insights of religious pioneers become luminous and convincing. The great religious seers have said that man is a spark of the divine, that the spirit of man is the candle of the Lord, that there is "that of God in every man." It is appropriate that the very first chapter of the first book of the Bible should contain the statement that God made man in His image and after His likeness. This is one of the basic premises of any truly spiritual religion without which such religion is impossible. Only a person who is in some sense a musician, though not necessarily a productive one, can appreciate music, and only a creature who is spiritual, and thus in some sense like God, can commune with God who is Spirit.

The perennial claim of religious leaders that they and all men have in them something akin to God can be made to seem amazingly presumptuous. It is either one of the deepest truths of the world or an evidence of man's colossal egotism. Those who have come to the latter conclusion have often suggested that other beasts, if they could think about the subject, would hold that God was

57

like them or that they were made in His likeness. But Montaigne and the many others who have written in this strain have failed to see the immense importance of the qualifying clause they are forced to attach. *If* the geese could think about the subject they would undoubtedly consider that they were made in the image of God and they might be quite right, for they would then be no longer geese, as we know geese; they would be spirits. Montaigne's famous geese who look out upon a goose-centered world, considering the nature of God and man, would be exactly what we mean by men. It is not the physical form of man that we most prize, a form which is, indeed, remarkably like that of other creatures. A creature concerned with his inner life and the nature of God would be a *spirit* quite regardless of such details as webbed toes and wings or erect posture and flexible hands. If we are guilty of anthropomorphism when we interpret the world in terms of the highest we know, i.e., the level of spirit, let us by all means cherish our anthropomorphism.

The ancient religious conviction that man is akin to God takes us beyond pessimism and optimism in the ordinary sense. The conviction is incompatible with a belief in total depravity, for if man has something of God's own Spirit in him he is never beyond redemption. No matter how wicked and selfish a person may be, our fundamental insight concerning man's nature keeps our hope alive. There is always something left to which appeal can be made, there is always an inner witness which is the powerful ally of any good force from the outside.

But the old belief in "that of God in every man" does not, on the other hand, entail a complete optimism about man in general or any particular man. The human heart is made in the image of God, as the Book of Genesis says, but it is also a continual forge of idols. Our very interest in our own inner states may become unwholesome and evil. The man who seeks self-approbation may become a moral prig. In other words, the conviction that in every man there is something of God gives us no certainty of success, and much less does it give certainty of failure; it gives us room for *hope*.

The implications of the notion of man's spiritual nature are as wide as the world, so far as our conduct toward other men is concerned. This basic idea affects our relation to the state, to its enemies, to the criminal, to the insane, to the education of children. Some of these special as-

59

pects of the subject will be mentioned in later chapters, but no book can deal with all of them, for they reach to every corner of human life. It follows, for example, that human souls are more important than anything else in the world, far more important than things, and that things derive their value from what they contribute to the development of that which is spiritual and divine in men.

Jesus, more than anyone who lived before him, enunciated clearly the transcendent value of every individual spirit. Jesus called to all those with a human form, no matter how desolate, discouraged, or evil, and said they were important in the sight of God. Each one, in the teaching of Jesus, is a child of God, and that fact is not affected by any accident of race, nation, age, sex, intelligence, or creed. "You are all children of God," he told men, "and you are of more value than many sparrows or even than the whole world." A full understanding and acceptance of this great teaching leads to a transvaluation of all values, to a recognition of the fact that it is necessary to lose your life in order to save it. This idea is older than Jesus, but who else made it so vivid and convincing? "He was the first to give it calm, simple, and fearless expression," says Harnack, "as though it were a truth which grew on every tree."[1]

The world view we are presenting, the world view of spiritual religions, is one which recognizes a deep and wide fissure in the cosmos. This fissure separates spirit from what is not spirit and, for the religious mind, it is the most significant chasm in the universe. Part of man is on one side of this chasm and part of him is on the other. He is the link between the two parts of the world, as the ancients said, and any sound religion will recognize clearly man's relation to this chasm. It is because he is partly on one side that he needs salvation, and it is because he is partly on the other side that he is capable of being saved.

The fact that man has a sense of sin and feels the need of salvation is truly remarkable. Man's sense of sin as a spiritual blemish utterly different from a mere mistake is one of the strongest evidences of his spiritual nature and one of the most striking results of his self-consciousness. That the sense of sin is uniquely human has been well argued,[2] and it is easy to show that the implications of this sense carry us far. Above all, the sense of sin is our ground of infinite hope. We

[1] Adolf Harnack, *What is Christianity?* London, 1904, p. 70.
[2] Cf. A. E. Taylor, *The Faith of a Moralist.* London, 1930.

cannot advance without great needs which demand satisfaction and we could hardly have salvation if the need for it were not felt.

When a human being condemns, not others, but himself, and not merely his individual acts, but the total self from which the acts have come, we catch a glimpse of another dimension than any found in the purely natural world. This spiritual longing and felt need of salvation are evidence of man's manifest dependence upon another world which seems to be impinging upon this world of things. This longing may be, as Professor Gilbert Murray has intimated,[3] simply the result of an old race instinct for which no object of satisfaction exists, but this is hard to believe of creatures on the human level. The suggestion receives its plausibility chiefly from the implied parallel between human acts and acts like those of lemmings. But we see that the analogy is delusive when we realize that self-conscious human life belongs to a totally different order than that of lemmings. In any case there is no doubting the fact of man's longing for salvation, and any creature with such a longing is profoundly spiritual in essence.

[3] Gilbert Murray, Essay on "Stoicism," in *Tradition and Progress*. Boston, 1922.

VI. Spiritual Salvation

The need for salvation rests upon a surprising and apparently enduring fact, the fact of contradiction in the inner life. We all tend to begin, as Socrates did, with the assumption that wickedness is a matter of ignorance, and we often hold that, if a man really knows what is good, he is sure to do it. If a man were completely convinced that friendship was more valuable than personal gain, would he ever sacrifice friendship to gain? Perhaps if he were logical he would not, but the fact is that all men have in them an illogical strain, the supreme illogicality of flat contradiction. It has been the experience of countless men that they have turned deliberately against the best they have known. The experience of St. Paul as recorded in the seventh chapter of the Epistle to the Romans is the classic example.

The supreme demand in all conduct is the demand for trustworthiness. As Bosanquet well said, "*Bona fides* is the ultimate need in all matters of conduct, and religion is the supreme *bona fides*."[1] In spiritual religion we assert that the fact of primary importance is the fact of our relationship to God, who is completely good, but we then *act* as though this were *not* the primary fact. This is the fundamental contradiction of life and is what we mean by sin. Sin, then, is far deeper than a matter of individual acts, and refers to a radical failure in veracity.

The religious man, believing as he does in the spiritual nature of God and in the spiritual nature of man, soon discovers that he has two selves. One self is the present actual self, narrow, confused, and self-contradictory; the other is the *real self* which a man may see but dimly, but which he soon realizes is his greatest possession. I am not *really* what I now appear to be, I am *bona fide* other, and my sin consists in the continual rejection and disownment of the *bona fide* other. Salvation consists in that change by means of which a man faithfully embraces his real self, overcomes the fundamental contradiction, and comes to the place where his heart is *really* given to the best he can conceive.

[1] Bernard Bosanquet, *What Religion Is*. London, 1920, p. 48.

There has been a marked tendency among religious leaders to feel that the word "saved" needs other words after it to make a complete sentence. They would answer the old question, "What must I do to be saved?" by adding another question, "Saved from what?" But when we try to answer this further question it is very hard to know what to say. We say from fear, from greed, from malice, from selfishness, but are these all? We may say from hell, but about hell we know very little. Perhaps it is better to follow the general practice of our race and use the word in the old absolute sense. We are *saved*, and that is all. This is the positive word, and other states may be defined in relation to salvation rather than vice versa. If you are saved you are in a condition in which your heart is really given to the best you can conceive, and that is a great positive experience. What, then, are you saved from? You are saved from everything else but that.

The condition most nearly the opposite of salvation is one of *waste*. Waste is the real tragedy in any avenue of life, and any thoughtful person is moved when he sees great powers which are either undeveloped or badly used. It is more than a truism that the saddest words are "it might

65

have been." If every divine propensity were to be used, if no essential part should atrophy, that would be salvation.

Salvation so conceived is something far deeper and more radical than moral change in the narrow sense of the word. Moral results follow, but the experience behind the moral change is fundamentally religious; it is akin to the supreme act of reverence or trust. There must be an inner spring behind and beneath the new conduct and this is another way of saying we must be born again. The change must be internal before it is external. A second birth is not something for the emotionally unstable, but is a healthy, wholesome, and normal human experience.

But how is a man saved? How can we be born anew? The message of Jesus, as well as of countless others, is that we can be saved only if we give ourselves away. This paradox is absolutely central to the spiritual life and may be illustrated without end. The person who is continually concerned about the state of his soul, and the moral progress he is making, is in an enterprise which is necessarily self-defeating. The enterprise is self-defeating because the religious man, as he watches his progress, feels that he has, for the time at least, succeeded; he supposes that he has achieved something of himself apart from the object of his trust. His very concern for the state of his soul is a species of selfishness, and selfishness is sin because it involves the act of giving ourselves to the partial rather than to the perfectly and completely good.

We are saved by giving ourselves away and the very act of trust will work wonders in a man's inner life that no amount of individual striving would accomplish. The central act of religion has reminded many of the experience of learning to swim in which a man, by trusting himself to the water, learns more than has been learned by all his previous hectic splashing.

We have many words for the experience which makes salvation possible, and it makes little difference which word we use. We are saved by *loyalty*, we are saved by *trust*, we are saved by *love*, we are saved by *caring*. All of these words refer to the same experience, the experience in which we hold something supreme and give ourselves unconditionally to it. The fact of unconditionality is crucial. I am not really loyal to my nation, if I am loyal to it under certain conditions; I do not really *trust* God unless I can say with Job, "Though he slay me, yet will I trust him"; I do not really love my son if I say I shall love

67

him as long as he loves me. Those of us who are pacifists have often criticized unintelligently the patriot's toast, "My country, right or wrong." The patriot is at liberty to distinguish between his country and his government, to criticize national policies, to refuse to obey immoral commands, but if he is really a patriot he will be steadfastly *loyal* in every situation, most loyal of all, perhaps, when his country seems to be going in the wrong direction and thus needing him most. Much of the wonder and glory of the start of a new home lies in the very completeness of the transaction; it is unconditional, it is not temporary. The word "if" does not appear in the marriage ceremony, and neither does it appear in the creed of the man who embraces spiritual religion. The act of giving ourselves is absolute or it is nothing.

The truth which is embodied in the religious use of such words as love, loyalty, and caring has long been summed up in the phrase "salvation by faith." It is an admirable phrase and indicates, on the part of religious thinkers, a sound psychology. Human nature, they have intimated, is peculiar in that it can be changed only by the principle of indirection. You cannot give a soul unity by finding a center within itself; you can give a soul unity only by directing all its powers to a center outside itself. If the person really *cares* for something other than himself in such a way that he will give himself to it unconditionally, he already has, without striving for it, a saved condition in his own spirit. Luther succeeded in part because of his sound psychology; he knew the secrets of the human heart. But has anyone ever stated this essential point in the religious life better than did Professor Bosanquet?

> We cannot be "saved" as we are; we cannot cease to be what we are; we can only be saved by giving ourselves to something in which we remain what we are, and yet enter into something new. The peculiar attitude in which this is effected is religious faith. And this is, as I see the matter, just what we mean by religion—this, and no more, but nothing less.[2]

It is easy to see how men impressed in a lively way with the psychological fact of man's inability to save himself, with the fact that his salvation comes from the outside, should come to think of it as an arbitrarily imposed gift. This is the essential Calvinistic approach to the question and is at least as true as the opposite error which supposes that man saves himself, but there is a truth which is far more precious than such half-truths.

[2] *Ibid.,* pp. 8, 9.

69

The precious truth is that there is a "double search," that the fundamental experience of religion is that in which both God and man are needed. Salvation does come from outside us, but it is not arbitrarily imposed; it comes only when we *give ourselves*. We are made new by the grace of God and by our own efforts, but the grace of God must not be looked upon as arbitrary. If the grace of God is arbitrary, He is not worthy of our reverence. When we are trying to learn to swim it is the water, to be sure, that holds us up, but the peaceful result occurs only when we first trust. We are saved by giving ourselves unconditionally, but it is within our power to give ourselves or not to give.

What is the place of Jesus Christ in the salvation on which any genuinely spiritual religion rests? Thousands have asserted that they have been saved "by his blood" or "in his Name." Sometimes these phrases have represented attempts to do justice to the fact that salvation comes from outside us, but they run the risk of seeming to say that we are saved by some external transaction, and this any spiritual religion is bound to reject. Our salvation is meaningless if it takes place anywhere except in our own spirits, for it is our spirits that need to be *saved*. A merely heavenly transaction will not suffice.

Often our words about salvation through Christ mean that the Person whom we meet in the Gospels is one who stirs us to the act of trust and loyalty on which salvation rests. We know that our wills need to be affected, that information will not suffice, and how are our wills affected if not by the magic of personality? If our relationship to Jesus is something deeper than a theory about His divinity, if it is relationship of personal discipleship that stirs us to the depths of our lives, we have there the kind of setting in which genuine salvation might well be expected. When we talk about salvation through Christ, therefore, we are referring not merely to a theory, but to an historical fact.

Leading exponents of spiritual religion have made much of the inner, or living, Christ. By this they have referred to the birth in each loving heart of the *very same* reality that was manifested in Jesus. Perhaps the best evidence that each man has in him something of what was perfectly in Jesus is that we respond so amazingly to what we find in Him. Christ really means something to us when he becomes more than an historical figure and is born today in our frail hearts.

The experience of Christ within helps us to see how it is that, though men are normally saved through Christ, there have been saved persons in all generations who have had no knowledge of the Carpenter of Nazareth. No human heart has been without an inner witness, no human heart has been without the living Christ, and the presence of this witness has made possible the culmination of the double search at all times. But why should we call this inner witness the "living Christ"? Why not call it the "inner light"? For centuries men have called it the "living Christ," because they found in a dim and confused way in themselves the *same* thing that they saw so beautifully portrayed in the Jesus of history. Men call things by the same name when it is obvious that they belong together.

Are men ever completely saved? The question is particularly difficult to answer because we all know ourselves best and we should hesitate to say that we are completely saved, for we are still conscious of elements of contradiction within us, and yet if we say complete salvation is not possible we seem to lack faith either in the power of God or in the capacities of men. In practice we have to say that there are degrees of salvation; though all men sin, some are more nearly loyal to their *bona fide* selves than others are. But if we assert the *necessity* of sin, we seem to be condoning it, and accepting defeat before the battle is fought. The position of spiritually-minded men on this subject, as on so many others in religion, is fundamentally paradoxical. The religious man in all generations says, "I am not fully saved, but by the grace of God I can be."

VII. Worship in Spirit and in Truth

The act of worship is the characteristic act of religion and the part of religion which is apparently easiest to see from the outside. That is, the outside observer can watch the individual as he kneels or bows and can hear him as he sings or chants. But we soon realize that the outside observer is only watching physical accompaniments of worship and the genuine inner act is beyond observation. Worship is far different from, and more important than, particular "acts of worship," since it goes forward with a great variety of such "acts" or even without them.

Many devoutly religious persons are quick to say that their moments of most genuine worship have often come without the use of incense, organ, sermon, or psalter. Perhaps the truest worship will come on a hillside when the individual is sitting alone watching the setting sun, perhaps it will come in a great railway station with the crowds of humanity milling about. What is the experience which men call worship and which seems to take on such diverse forms?

In the first place, we can say that worship may be described as a *mood*. This mood may find expression in words, but need not; it may be enhanced by artistic aids, but it can be most pronounced without them. Worship is not merely an intellectual response, and not merely an emotional response, but an experience in which the whole soul is lifted up and acts as a unit. It is well known that many delicate flavors delight us because of their subtle combination of opposites. This helps us to understand the mood of worship because it combines two moods which are as different as any could well be, the mood of awe and the mood of childlike trust.

One of the most striking evidences that worship is made up of these apparently conflicting elements is seen in the recorded prayer of Jesus which begins, "I thank thee, O Father, Lord of Heaven and Earth." Here is a recognition of God as the Creator of the great universe, the One who made Orion and the Seven Stars. The normal result of the thought of God as Creator is a sense of man's smallness in view of the immensity about him.

We are filled with adoration, we experience what Professor Otto has called the "mysterium tremendum." But Jesus places by the side of all this the balancing thought of God as Father. Here we have a sense of the friendliness of the world, of the importance of each one of us because the kindly care of each one of us is a corollary of the Fatherhood of God. Just as the mood of wonder and awe increases the sense of the littleness of man, the mood of friendly and childlike trust increases the sense of the importance of man in the scheme of things, because of his heavenly kinship.

Religion at its best is always a matter of paradox and this is illustrated nowhere better than in the mood of worship. Wonder without trust is enfeebling, and trust without wonder is sentimental, but the two together produce a mood which is the highest that men know. We are reminded of the height of a great Gothic cathedral which is made possible by the fact that the central arches and the flying buttresses push against each other. The loftiness of worship is possible because of the thrust and counterthrust of wonder and love.

It is certainly true that many persons, who lack specific and definite belief in God, are nevertheless well acquainted with the mood of worship.

Their highest experiences have the religious quality about them even if the thought of immediate communion with God who is Spirit is meaningless to them. Worship, then, is broader in its scope than belief, and it is probable that there is no single living person who is not, at some time or other, touched by this high mood. Perhaps if people will allow this mood to become dominant in their lives the deeper experiences of communion with God will follow. Many in the past have learned that the experience of worship is a precious thing which leads them far when it is cherished and cultivated.

How can this high mood be cultivated? In one sense we must say the Spirit bloweth where it listeth, and that we must wait for it, and yet experience has shown that the mood is more likely to come in some settings than others. We cannot work the miracle, but we can at least make ourselves ready for the miracle to happen. This is the real reason for church services. Every reasonable minister knows that the items arranged in the order of service are not synonymous with worship, but he hopes they may *facilitate* worship. Great music, harmoniously constructed buildings, ancient words; all these help. The sense of life's paradox, of the strangeness and the familiarity, comes best to many persons in the presence of beauty. Perhaps this is because beauty itself combines familiarity and strangeness. The hymn uses the same old sounds that appear in our narrow scale every day, but the familiar sounds are strange because they are arranged in a new pattern. The church has bricks and stones like those we see every day, but they have been arranged, first in the thought of the architect and then by the hand of workmen, into meaningful and balanced forms.

The ancient words aid us because they are so familiar and yet are not our own. It was a sound instinct which led men to use ancient tongues in worship. It made little difference whether they used old Latin or the quaint English of the King James Version and the Book of Common Prayer. Language that is completely new has only one dimension. It is a significant fact that many persons who are devoutly religious, and yet unable to believe the old creeds, nevertheless wish, in the hour of worship, to repeat the old phrases without change. By their act they are showing that they realize worship has more than mere intellectual content.

A clear statement of the position just mentioned is that furnished in the writings of Pro-

78

fessor Kirsopp Lake. He accepts the old words liturgically but not scientifically.

The creeds which were not taken into the liturgy have irrevocably perished, but those which are recited in the services of the church live on. It is this liturgical character which is often forgotten. Not a few of my friends often object to me that they cannot understand how any one can wish to remain in a church which has a creed that he does not believe. They obviously cannot; but this is largely because they look on a creed as a theological document,— and as nothing more—while we more often regard it as an integral part of an extraordinarily beautiful work of art as well as of theology,—the Christian liturgy. It is perfectly true that the theology of this liturgy is quite alien to mine, or to that of any Experimentalist. So is the theology of those who built Durham Cathedral. Nevertheless the liturgical art of the services of the church—like the architectural art of its cathedrals, rouses a response in me which cannot be wakened by any modern service or by any modern building, even though its theology may be irreproachably up-to-date.[1]

The argument of Professor Lake has its aspects of danger, and such a practice as he upholds will surely seem dishonest to many, though his own honesty is beyond reproach. His argument from the architectural parallel is singularly telling. We should be most foolish to shut out any-

[1] Kirsopp Lake, *The Religion of Yesterday and To-morrow.* Boston, 1926, p. 101.

one from participation in a liturgical tradition when such participation is sincerely craved.

If our religious services overemphasize the intellectual aspect, they destroy the mood of worship. It is unfortunately true that many churches come to be places of instruction and little more. The people who attend them may learn many facts, but they are not likely to be caught up into a mood that elevates them to new levels. It is obvious that conduct is often quite unchanged by mere intellectual assent, but a general mood is so deep-going that it must eventually affect an individual in countless ways. It is not important that little children should understand what is said by the minister, but it is highly important that the adults about him should be genuinely reverent, for the mood of reverence goes over to the child, even without his knowing it.

One of the most surprising facts about what ordinarily passes for worship is the little use we make of silence. Silence seems to be the normal response of the individual who has had a really ennobling experience, and this is well seen in many picture galleries where the rule about quietness is superfluous. In our best moments we all realize that the really great things cannot be said and that we only look foolish when we try to say them. Our lives are, for the most part, full of noise and bustle and hurry, and it is certainly clear that our service of worship should be remarkable by contrast. The "snappy" service in which "something is doing every moment" is too much like the great noisy world outside. If a university is a place "where nothing useful is taught," why may not a church be a place "where nothing *practical* is said?"

Individuals in all ages have known the value of quietness, they have prayed to the Father who heareth in secret, but there has been, in the Church as a whole, surprisingly little use of corporate silence. It is almost as though men were afraid of one another or of themselves; many would feel uncomfortable in a church if nothing were said for ten minutes. But why should they feel uncomfortable? Does God cease to speak because the minister ceases to speak? Every minister knows that there are times when his words are poor and thin, the repetition of platitudes, and why would it not be better in that case to have no words? At least, then, there would be nothing to *hinder* the search of the individual soul for God's presence. Probably the truth is that the leaders of corporate worship are afraid; they are afraid to depend on the still small voice; they put out their hands to steady the ark. We ask, in our vocal prayers, that God may speak to us, and then we do not wait to listen.

Worship, at its best, is a group experience. The individual on the lonely hillside may know the real presence of God, but there he is only one, and there are many to assert that, when they are with a company, each individual is more than himself. If there is any reality in the group idea, if there is any experience in which men become knit together into an organic whole and cease to be independent units like marbles in a bag, we should expect to find this deeper unity in worship. The very faces of the other persons present can help us; they can fill us with a new sense of the similarity of our problems and the common elements of our human nature. That is why an ordinary service of worship is so different from the experience of sitting alone at home listening to a sermon over the radio. As we listen to the radio we are not *participators*, but in every real service of worship each person contributes to the total mood, by the very expression on his face if in no other way. It is not uncommon for thoughts and hopes to be generated in an hour of group worship that are larger than, and different from, the combined thoughts and hopes of the various individuals on entering the building. When this happens worship is really *creative*. A true service of worship is probably the best example in the world of how a whole can be greater than the sum of its parts.[2]

If we begin to see how worship may be a creative group enterprise we soon realize that every effort at worship is an exciting venture. Such worship may have an order of service, but it certainly will not be a recital of what has already been learned. It is not like the playing of a phonograph record. If each person, including the minister, were to go to the service of worship full of expectancy and wonder, realizing that a creative venture was about to be undertaken in which the total result was quite unpredictable, then we would be justified in talking about that worship which is "in spirit and in truth."

We must never allow ourselves to think that worship is a matter of an experience that comes one day a week, one time a day, or in one particular place. There can be genuine worship in very ugly places where there is no architectural charm and there can be worship in the midst of daily toil. If we are to be men we must work as well as

[2] Readers interested in this important aspect of worship will be rewarded by a careful consideration of *Creative Worship*, by Howard Brinton. London, 1931.

worship, and the secret of the spiritual life lies in carrying over the spirit of worship into the common tasks of everyday life. Prayer is one specialized form of worship and the secret of prayer lies not in particular words, but in a prayerful spirit which can accompany one through the day. If, as we go to our jobs, travel on street cars, dig in the soil, and work in houses, we can have a continual sense of the wonder of existence, of the tragedy and deep comedy of human life about us, of the mystery and yet the familiarity of the great bustling world; life then becomes amazingly rich and fine. There are some who approximate this mood and yet do not think they are believers, and there are those who call themselves believers who hardly know what we mean when such a mood is mentioned. That religion which is spiritual religion begins with this high mood of continual worship and, as it is sustained, men become conscious of a Presence in their midst.

VIII. The Extension of the Sacramental

In our discussion of worship we have pointed out that no *particular* form is necessary for either the production or the expression of the worship which is in spirit. God does not dwell in temples made with hands, and the sense of the reality of God's presence is not dependent on any special physical act or group of acts. The person who experiences spiritual religion may know God in music or in silence, with spoken or unspoken prayers, with the Eucharist or without it, and, on the other hand, a person may have all the outward helps in the world without once having a vivid sense of God's real presence. Thus we may say that no particular outward aid is indispensable and that likewise no particular outward aid is sufficient in and of itself.

The understanding of the truth just stated is highly important in spiritual religion, but it must be carefully guarded or it will say too much. The

fact that no *particular* outward aid is necessary
does not mean that *no* outward aid is necessary.
Indeed, so long as we have bodies, we cannot be
free from physical stimuli and we can never escape from *some* physical media for spiritual experiences. If we leave off written prayer we may have
silent prayer, but the latter is as much a medium
as the former. There is always some physical
stimulus, whether it be the sight of the setting
sun, the smell of flowers that grew at home, the
sound of an old hymn, or the touch of another's
hand. We are not angels, we are men, and it is no
disgrace to suppose that we must employ physical
means to reach our highest spiritual levels. If we
despise physical media, and strive to arrive at spiritual levels independent of *all* physical helps, we
are committing what may be termed "the angelis-
tic fallacy."

A right understanding of man's status in creation midway between angels (if there are any)
and beasts makes clear the necessity of a sacramental view. Beasts have no sacraments because
they are only physical, and angels would have no
sacraments because they would be only spiritual,
but man's life is normally sacramental because he
is both physical and spiritual. A sacrament is a
physical means to a spiritual end. All spiritual re-

ligion is genuinely sacramental and, historically in Christianity, stresses the communion service rather than the office of preaching.

For the person devoted to spiritual religion the sacraments are windows through which the glory of God shines into human hearts. Wine becomes much more than the juice of the grape; it becomes an open door to the presence of the Eternal. Sacraments can have this high value even for little children who are sometimes carried to new levels as they watch their parents in the performance of sobering acts though they are absolutely untouched by preaching or praise. Clearly the whole sacramental idea reaches something true and fine in human life. It is psychologically correct.

We may accept the sacramental view of religion and yet leave unanswered the vitally practical question *how many* sacraments there are and *what* these are. Christians have been sorely divided on these questions: the Roman Church maintaining that the sacraments are seven, the ordinary Protestants recognizing but two,[1] and some Protestants recognizing three. These last include the act of washing one another's feet along with baptism and

[1] Cf. "The Articles of Religion," Article XXV. It is here specifically said that "Confirmation, Penance, Orders, Matrimony, and extreme Unction are not to be counted for Sacraments of the Gospel."

the Eucharist. It is hard to see why the act of foot-washing has not been adopted by all Christians, since it symbolizes one of the most important features of the teaching of Jesus and was certainly commanded by Him if the others were commanded. The Church of Rome has had the wisdom to make its sacraments deal chiefly with the great moments in any life, birth, adolescence, marriage, and death.

If the sacramental view of life is correct, the Roman Church would seem to have a distinct advantage over the ordinary Protestant Church in recognizing *more* sacraments. Is not the entrance into matrimony as holy and wonderful an experience as the entrance into the Church? If the latter is signalized by the sacrament of baptism, why should not the former be signalized by the sacrament of matrimony? It should be said that in all devout circles, Catholic or Protestant, matrimony is *actually* seen as a sacrament quite regardless of what church doctrine may say.

But if it becomes clear that the Roman view of what is sacramental is superior to the Protestant, does it not also become clear that there is no need to stop where Rome stops? Why should there be only seven any more than only two? Why not seventy times seven, as Jesus would surely have said?

Life becomes rich and fine if the great moments, like birth and marriage, are seen as windows through which God's light is streaming, but these great or potentially great moments are legion. The sacramental experience may be the reading of a true book; it may be the entrance into a deep friendship; it may be the undertaking of a journey. The holy time may be that in which a little child starts off to his first day of school, and many of us know that few times are as full of meaning. Some of us can never watch the beginning of a new home and the fine courage which so often dignifies the love of two young people without feeling that we have, indeed, looked into the Holy of Holies. Perhaps that is because the experience of falling in love is so closely analogous to the central experience of religion.

The point is, then, that when we limit the sacraments to any prescribed number we are doing violence to reality as we know it. The sacrament of cleaning a room is as genuine as the sacrament of penance and the true book is more than a book, just as wine is more than wine. A great library is as much a holy place as any high altar, and if we lift our hats when passing the building which houses the latter, why should we not lift our hats when passing the building that houses the former?

89

If we allow ourselves to think what a library means, if we dwell on the multitude of thoughts, the hours of patient literary labor, the uncounted efforts to pass on to us something of the mystery of living, we do indeed find ourselves by a magnificent window with the glory streaming through.

What is holy water? Is it water blessed by a priest? Or is it possibly the water that some poor, overworked woman uses to keep the clothes of her children clean so that they can go to school in decency and have in their lives the things denied her? What is holy bread? Is it bread that has been on an altar over which words have been said and sung? Or is the holiest bread that which some man earns by hard labor that those for whom he cares may eat? There may be sacraments more genuine than any which men in long robes ever know.

The gist of the matter is that a full acceptance of spiritual religion entails the abolition of the secular. There is no part of life that is *necessarily* secular, and our task is to see to it that no part is thus removed from the area of the sacred. Certain sections of the Christian Church have long made a sharp distinction between the religious life and the common life, the former often being identical with the monastic. The assumption is that a

man cannot attain to the highest religious standard if he has wife and children and carries on ordinary work in the ordinary world. This assumption we are bound to reject. Of course the tempta-
tions of ordinary life are great, but the tempta-
tions of monastic life are great also, and, in any
case, the acceptance of a double standard cannot
but have an evil influence. If men in common life
are told that they cannot expect to achieve real
spirituality, if they are assured that the married
state is less noble than that of celibacy, they will
cease to strive for the highest. Our danger is that
we shall be complacent about failure, and the
preaching of a double standard makes for com-
placency. We must hold, then, that there is only
one standard, that of Christ, and that it is for *all*
men. The "hard" sayings of Jesus are not merely
for those who are retired from the world, but
for those who must seek their salvation *in* the
world. Any occupation is a holy office if it serves
in any way, material or otherwise, to a fuller
realization of the spiritual vocation of man. John
Woolman's holy office was that of a tailor.

A good illustration of how common things may
be lifted to the sacramental level is that of the
daily mail. By means of our far-flung postal system people all over the earth are able to keep in

touch with those whom they love and have communion with them. Is not many a visit to a humble mailbox a daily mass? It is wonderful to think how radiant life could be if those who share in such common tasks and services could see how sacramental they really are.

Men have shown keen insight in recognizing the power there is in a sacred meal. The great end is the welding of many hearts into one, and eating together is one of the chief ways in which this miracle takes place. Let us, then, use this amazing means of enhancing the spiritual life, but why should we limit ourselves to a special ceremonial meal? Why should we not make every meal a Lord's Supper? If always when we eat we have a deep sense of the human lives whose scattered efforts have brought the food to us, if we always remember Jesus and his infinite compassion, then common food has already become more than food. Many of us can remember crackers and tea, or ordinary boiled potatoes, for that matter, that constituted a genuine Lord's Supper. All that we know of the general teaching of Jesus indicates, not that Jesus proposed to institute a fixed and necessary ceremonial, but that he wanted his friends to "remember" him when they ate together. If we are his disciples we, too, should remember him when we eat, morning, noon, and night. What we need is not less of the Eucharist but more, vastly more.

All who share in the efforts to maintain a spiritual religion are believers in the doctrine of "the real presence," but this real presence is not, for them, limited to what may be placed in a chalice. The Living Christ is genuinely present to the seeking soul, not symbolically or figuratively, but in *reality*. He is to the seeking soul far more real and more truly present than chairs and tables are. This is beautifully depicted by J. Doyle Penrose in his painting called "The Presence in the Midst." The setting of the picture is the old English meetinghouse at Jordans, where William Penn is buried, and near which is the scene of Gray's *Elegy*. A few plain people are gathered in silence in the old meetinghouse in which there is no music, no liturgy, and no incense. There is not even any speaking in this particular gathering, but high over the heads of the devout worshipers is the figure of Christ. The doctrine of the real presence has become for these people, the artist suggests, more than a doctrine; it has become a fact. A careful understanding of that picture helps us to know the difference between *ceremonial* and *sacramental*.

After we have become committed to the notion

of the sacrament of common life we are likely to go on and say that everything in the world is sacramental, but, if we do, we run the risk of effacing the distinction between good and evil. It is one thing to say that the sacraments are legion, but it is quite another to say that every individual thing is holy. We run the risk, then, of being falsely romantic about the world, or pantheistic. As a matter of fact there is filth in the world and there are filthy men. There are acts which are base and deceitful. There are men who are so eager to rise in the world that they make other men into stepping-stones, quite regardless of the result on the other lives. When one man "uses" another, is there anything sacramental about that? We have all repeated Tennyson's words about the flower in the crannied wall, but, if fully pressed, does not this notion obliterate distinctions of value? Does the pestilence-bearing rat shout the Creator's praise as fully and truly as does the full-throated songbird?

The considerations just mentioned make us realize that we must hold the idea of the sacrament of common life with some qualifications; we must hold it in such a way that we do not neglect distinctions in value, for the sense of value is itself holy. We may say that some aspects of life are much clearer windows than others, and yet we need not give up our first insight completely. The wonder of life consists in this—that, though things are in themselves evil, they can become instruments of great good. It is not suggested that this is a complete solution of the problem of evil, but it is undoubtedly true that many horrible experiences have become deeply sacramental. We know persons who have had new insights into the richness of life after the death of a much-loved child. We know many who have been struck by a loathsome disease and yet have so lived through the misery that the very disease has become an instrument of God's grace. That is another way of saying it has become a sacrament. It is our task to oppose evil, but God, by His great mercy, is clearly able to lead us on to new heights by means of evil experiences if we are willing to open our lives to the divine influence. There is, then, a very deep sense in which anything at all can become an instrument for the enhancement of the life of the spirit.

The sacramental idea is a sound one and is central to any spiritual religion, but we do violence to the very notion of a sacrament when we limit the notion to a few aspects of experience. As our religion becomes genuinely spiritual we find that we are surrounded by open windows on every side and the light of God's countenance is streaming through all of them. Then the humble tasks of everyday life are lifted up and we cannot but go every step of the way in genuine reverence. If we were to remove our shoes on all holy ground, they would be removed all the time. If a man begins by being a sacramentalist, it is difficult to see how he can avoid going that far. There is no logical stopping place between the notion that *some things* are sacramental and the notion that *all things* are potentially sacramental. But, above all, we must make it clear that the view of the sacraments which this chapter has championed is not one which would hinder any devout person in his devotion to fixed forms. We may agree with T. Edmund Harvey that "what we need is to realize and to claim the liberty by which a hundred forms may become sacramental, and not to deny the reality of the life which may underlie the fixed forms which others use."[2] It is hoped that those who have cherished the few sacraments which the

[2] T. Edmund Harvey, *A Wayfarer's Faith* (London, 1920, p. 76). The reader interested in this conception of the sacraments may consult with profit Chapters IV and V of Mr. Harvey's book. See also Joan M. Fry, *The Communion of Life* (London, 1910), and A. Barratt Brown, *Wayside Sacraments* (London, 1932).

Church has stressed may continue to cherish them and, at the same time, consider carefully the fundamental idea back of all sacraments. The extension of the area of the sacramental will be the natural result.

IX. The Continuity of Revelation

That God has spoken directly to men has been accepted as a fact by countless generations of religious persons. This is what has been meant by the emphasis on revealed religion, as apart from merely natural religion. Man has, indeed, had desires and tendencies within himself which have helped to produce what we call religion, but this is not all; at the same time, so it has been devoutly believed, God has contributed to the total result by His own self-revelation. The religious spirit has not been the desire of the moth for the star, but has been a "double search."[1]

Now it must be said that the question of the validity of this claim cannot be lightly dismissed. The claim does not include a logical impossibility, and it has certainly been made by thousands of persons who earn our full respect. Indeed, if we

[1] Cf. Rufus M. Jones, *The Double Search*. Philadelphia, 1906.

accept the argument concerning the spiritual nature of God and the spiritual nature of man, is not direct spiritual commerce between them just what we should expect? It is easier, really, to believe that God would reveal His nature to a human spirit than to believe a stone would reveal its nature to the same spirit, and yet all of us tacitly accept the self-revelation of the stone. There may be times, in the midst of philosophical discussion, when we doubt the independent reality of the stone and claim the experience of it is entirely subjective, but it is easy to show that no sane man lives by such a belief. In practice, at least, we are incurable realists.

The person who doubts the reality of an objective divine revelation is likely to urge the consideration that direct commerce between God and man is impossible because the two are so different. But to this it is sufficient to reply that all knowledge implies a relation between the unlike. The paradox of knowledge is that it is impossible unless the knower and the known have something in common, but that it is likewise impossible unless the knower and the known are genuinely different.[2] In the characteristic knowing relation we

[2] Cf. A. Seth Pringle-Pattison, *Balfour Lectures on Realism.* Edinburgh, 1933.

deal with what is distant in time and place, and thus, by means of knowledge, we always "get outside of our own skins."[3] The knowledge of the self-revealing God is no more of a miracle than the knowledge of sticks and stones. Both are open to hallucination and illusion, but there is no reason why either should be rejected on general principles.

The task of spiritual religion is to show, not that revelation is to be denied, but to show the necessity of the extension of the concept. It has often been assumed that God once spoke directly to men, but that the time came when this ended arbitrarily, since which time men have only known God at second hand. The theory of the inspiration of the Bible has been taught in this way for generations, but the theory is not defensible. If we accept the teaching of Jesus about the nonlocal character of God, it is hard to suppose that God would limit the revelation of Himself to a particular time and place.

But it can also be shown that the notion of a completely external revelation is self-defeating. If the revelation is completely foreign to our ex-

[3] I know of no statement of the significance of knowledge more attractive than that found in the concluding paragraphs of A. O. Lovejoy's, *The Revolt Against Dualism*. Chicago, 1930.

perience, how do we recognize it when we are told of it? In knowledge we may have commerce with an *object* in some sense alien to ourselves, as was shown above, but we cannot understand an *experience* utterly alien to any we have had. This is well illustrated in our efforts to make the congenitally blind understand what we mean by color. The blind person can understand the raised letters R E D, and he can understand the analogy of a loud noise, but these are not the experience of *color*. Knowledge by description is effective only when it is a means whereby we point to knowledge by *acquaintance*. Unless a person has already had the experience of direct revelation of God, he cannot even understand what the prophets of the past mean when they speak of such direct revelations. The acceptance of the fact of revelation at *any* time implies, then, the fact of revelation now. A somewhat different, but supplementary point was well made by Josiah Royce:

Unless there is something in our individual experience which at least begins to bring us into a genuine touch, both with the fact that we need salvation and with the marks whereby we may recognize the way of salvation, and the essentially divine process, if such there be, which alone can save—unless, I say, there is within each one of us something of this interior light by which saving divine truth is to be discerned, religious insight is impossible, and then no merely external revelation can help us.[4]

The Bible, as a record of direct illumination, is a great help to us, but not as something external. The Bible can be of real aid only if the reader has within himself the experiences to which the Biblical writers point. A revelation which was completely of the past would be a useless revelation, and the Bible means more if revelation is continuous. The ideal situation is that in which the inner and the outer revelations buttress, supplement, and check each other.

Though so many have claimed to believe in a closed revelation, their practice has belied their words. That the Reformers, with their great emphasis on the Bible and their rejection of later accumulations, really believed in continuous revelation is shown by their creedal statements, confessions, and *interpretations* of Scripture. Moreover, the use of the Prayer Book indicates that people consider it inspired, and well they may, for many of the collects of the Book of Common Prayer are certainly on a par with Biblical material. The hymns are extensions of the Psalter and are continually going through the sifting

[4] Josiah Royce, *Sources of Religious Insight*. New York, 1912, p. 26.

process which the psalms once underwent before the canon was established. The weekly practice of most Christians in worship indicates their real conviction that the canon of Scripture is still open. The very notion of a Finis in the field of Scripture is a fundamental impiety.

This does not mean that we must reject the notion of a canon. It is a great help to the common man to know in advance what writings have received the stamp of approval of sensitive men and, if this help is provided, some things must be ruled out. The canon cannot reasonably be opposed in that it is negative, for any standard is negative in that it rules some things out, but the canon should be opposed if it is arbitrary in its negativity or provides for rejection before a fair estimate can be made. Most of us are glad that the apocryphal Gospels were ruled out by the early Christians, and we should reject most of our current literature. The point is, not that there should be no canon, but that there should be no *closed canon.*

The rejection of the notion of a closed canon does not entail the further notion that all times have been equally important for the education and salvation of the human spirit. All we are bound to reject is an artificial temporal limitation. We should be quick to admit that there have been single centuries more significant for the race than entire millennia. On the whole it is good that the Bible stresses the time and place it does stress, for the Hebrew people were a people of spiritual genius and the time of the incarnation was certainly a flowering time for the human spirit. Not all men are equally valuable in the alleged revelations that come to them and it is quite right to emphasize the insights of the spiritual giants. The Bible as we have it includes more of these giants than does any other collection of literature in the world. If men were to fasten on one collection of books and respect it fanatically, it is hard to think of a more fortunate choice.

The dim recognition, on the part of the multitude, of the necessity of dependence on the person with prophetic insight is probably part of the reason for the tenacity with which men in all generations have held to Scriptures. Another reason for the hold of Scriptures on the average man has been the wholesome respect for written words which so many people have felt. It is no wonder that words have seemed holy. Written language is an almost miraculous link between generations, making possible the continuance of civilization with its vicarious profit from the experiences of

others. When we consider what life would be like
without books, we are not surprised that *some*
books have seemed holy; the wonder is that li-
braries have not been our common shrines.

The exponent of a spiritual religion cherishes
the Scriptures of his race, but he does so in a particular way. As we look at the books which are
revered by Christians, collected together under
the name *Holy Bible*, we soon see that these books
are most unequal. This, of course, is what we
should expect, since we know they were written
by many men throughout a period of many centuries. The fundamental insights recorded are not
all compatible with each other, and we are forced
to choose between them. The moral standards
range from those of revenge, in which the actual
harm of the other is desired, to the ennobling love
of the Gospels. Parts of the Bible are very crude,
parts give expression to primitive science which
we have learned to discard, but other parts include
high poetry and devotional literature that have
never been surpassed. Many of the psalms really
speak to the conditions of men in all times.

How may we decide what material to include
in our canon? This is only a variant of the question how we know what revelations are authentic.
The moment we understand that many claims

THE ESSENCE OF SPIRITUAL RELIGION

have been made, we see at once that we must have a criterion of judgment. How do we know that the Bible is inspired and the Koran is not? Why do we reject the claims of the Mormons and the Shakers?[5] Clearly we all assume that a mere claim of supernatural sanction on the part of the authors is not enough to satisfy us.

Since the time of Coleridge it has been the fashion to say that the Bible is inspired because it "finds" us. The assumption is that we already have in us a more or less unexpressed knowledge of God, and that what we find in the Bible matches this. Whatever reason we may give finally boils down to this position. If we say we accept revelation because some other person or persons have accepted it, we must finally answer the question why we accept the opinion of the other persons, and that can only be because they, too, "find" us.[6] We are justified in calling writing inspired if it

[5] The history of the rise and decline of the Shaker movement is most instructive to the student of religion. The claim of direct revelation was made with great confidence, especially in the period just a century ago. The very title of the chief Shaker book of the period is arresting: *A Holy, Sacred and Divine Roll and Book from the Lord God of Heaven to the Inhabitants of Earth.* This was no more extreme on one side than the notion of a closed canon was extreme on the other.
[6] This introduces the question of authority, which is the subject of the next chapter. As will be shown there, the exponent of spiritual religion is by no means a mere individualist.

has gone beyond the temporary and local in such a way that it speaks to man *qua* man. This happens only when the author is in touch with fundamental reality. Our canon should include that material on which men may safely depend for spiritual strength.

We can never say exactly to what extent an author is expressing his own feeble ideas and to what extent God has spoken through him. There is a sense in which every true book seems to its author to be the work of Another; he writes better than he knows; he feels he is used by a Power greater than himself. This is especially true in poetic creation and the best of the Bible is on the level of poetry. Unless we reject the reality of God, there would seem to be no good reason for rejecting the most obvious explanation of this common experience.

Much that "finds" us is outside the ordinary Bible. This would include different material for each one of us and sometimes our selections would surprise others.[7] Probably each man has some pas-

---

[7] The writings which thus speak to men are not always avowedly religious ones by any means. It may be surprising that there are men who would include parts of *Pickwick* in their private canons. It is surprising, also, to see how some persons cling to a bit of writing which seems to most men to be bad writing. Great ideas have been transferred by feeble instruments.

sage of prose or poetry to which he returns again and again because it speaks to his condition and gives him new courage for the task of living.

In practice each man has both a *longer* and a *shorter* Bible. Our longer Bible includes much, from many traditions, that lies outside the familiar black leather covers, and the longer Bibles of no two persons are identical. In the same way we have shorter Bibles, because, within the familiar black covers, there are some passages which "find" us while others never can. Perhaps your shorter Bible includes the truly reverent Psalms, some lucid passages from the Prophets, all the recorded words of Jesus, and parts of the letters of Paul. And just as no two longer Bibles are identical, so no two shorter Bibles are identical either. Some men make theirs with scissors and paste, but probably most men make theirs unconsciously.

As soon as we expand our notion of inspiration and make longer Bibles we are already near the position sponsored by the Roman Catholic Church, by means of which it hopes to take advantage of new inspiration which has come since the Bible was written. The chief trouble in practice, with this conception, is the fact that it, too, tends to *limit* immediate revelation. Revelation, for the Roman Catholic, is practically limited to one particular channel which he calls the Church. From the point of view of spiritual religion the only trouble with the Catholic Church is that it is not sufficiently "catholic." It does not have a sufficiently lively sense of the many channels through which God speaks to men; it is not able to take advantage, in any normal way, of the profound insights of those who may be quite outside the Church tradition. Perhaps what is needed is an enlargement of the notion of the Church.

The ordinary Catholic view of inspiration and revelation is far superior to the ordinary Protestant view, but there is a larger and truer view than either one as ordinarily stated, a view that is really implicit in the religious acts of good Protestants and Catholics alike. This is the view of expectancy. God has spoken, but He has not ceased to speak, and He is not limited in His revelation by the fences which men set up. New light may break forth at any time and is breaking forth wherever devout spirits learn to wait on the Lord. This is a world of emerging novelty, and God may speak to men in ways of which we have not dreamed. This, at least, is the view of revelation inherent in all spiritual religion.

X. The Basis of Spiritual Authority

Sooner or later, all who attempt to be intelligently religious must reckon with the dilemma of authority. The dilemma arises out of the smallness of the sphere of experience to which every individual is limited. Since our own experience is so slight, and since it may so easily be illusory within its own area, we seek the opinion of others to enlarge our boundaries. If we do not depend upon others, we find there are few things of which we are at all certain. Thus we seem driven to a dependence upon authority, but as soon as we ask *which* authority, we see that the other horn of the dilemma is equally difficult. If we do depend upon others, how do we know we are justified in doing so? If we say we depend upon authority because it has proved to be in line with our experience, are we not right back in our limited area again?

This dilemma is not unlike that which faces the

logician who attempts to uphold induction. If we have counted all the cases, no inference is necessary since we already have the desired information, and if we do not count all the cases, it is hard to see how inference is justified since those not counted may have characteristics different from the characteristics of those counted.

The paradox of authority, which is akin to the central paradox of religion, is that a being so frail and ignorant as to need to depend on an authority external to himself should recognize the merits of authority when he is introduced to it. All of us, in practice, solve the dilemma by accepting the paradox, holding that we have within us latent capacities which are so aroused by a sufficient external stimulus that we are at least able to follow when we cannot initiate.

That we must depend upon authority in order to live is obvious and therefore we may say that all men in practice believe in authority, regardless of what they may say. If we were to limit our action to what we know by immediate experience we could hardly move. Most of us cannot test our automobiles to see whether they are safely constructed, and none of us is willing to drink poison to see whether it is deadly. It is clear that some

III

phases of life do not lend themselves to the method of constant verification.

Those who decry dependence upon authority, and advocate what they suppose is the scientific method of life, seem to forget that a complete renunciation of authority would entail a complete renunciation of civilization. If we could never take the wisdom of our predecessors as our starting point, if we had to make every discovery *de novo*, we should be reduced to a level of low savagery or less. Man, fortunately, is the creature who can profit in an almost limitless way by the advances of his race and thus save himself the necessity of personal experiment. Civilization is possible because men depend on the authority of their ancestors and thus are able to stand on the shoulders of these very ancestors.

Man has been fitted for cumulative progress by virtue of a nice balance between authority and experiment. A creature who depended entirely upon the authority of the past could not make progress since there would be no new discoveries, but neither would a creature make progress who *rejected* entirely the authority of the past. Such a creature would start at the bottom of the cultural ladder in each individual life and, though he might learn something in his lifetime, what he learned would not be passed on. The animals other than man are much closer to inventive spirit than they are to the spirit which profits vicariously by what others have thought or done and thus extends the area of experience.

The idea has somehow gained credence that authority and reason are antithetical. This could only be true if authority were followed in an absolutely blind fashion. On the contrary, it seems obvious that dependence upon authority is the most reasonable procedure possible in those areas of experience which do not admit of exact verification. How could we ever verify, except in a crudely figurative sense, the statement that the first duty of man is the love of God? It is hard to see how scientific method can even deal with the subject. In the same way we cannot verify the statement that the Parthenon is great art. It is surely reasonable for me to buttress and check my own conclusions on these matters by a careful and respectful consideration of the opinions of those whom I have learned to respect.

Perhaps the hardest question of all is always the question *which* expert we shall trust, for often, indeed, the doctors disagree. But even here we do not give up the method of reason. We do not choose one authority arbitrarily or because we like his complexion. There is always a reason why one should be selected rather than another and usually there are many reasons. An important reason is the ability of the authorities to appeal to many sides of our natures at once and thus to make us "trust" them. They appeal to us because, like the Bible, they "find" us at our deeper levels. This aspect of the problem has been admirably expressed by Archbishop Temple in his Gifford Lectures.

It is important to remember that there is no contrast between Reason and Authority. It is impossible to accept a belief on Authority except so far as the Authority is accepted by Reason. In so far as a child's acceptance of what he is told is totally uncritical, that is not acceptance on Authority, but on the causal action of impressions received. His belief rests on Authority only when his acceptance of what he is told is due to trust in those who tell.[1]

In the experience of *trust* we are in an area which is neither that of the irrational nor that of the necessarily true. In other words, trust where there is not a shadow of a doubt is not trust, and, in a similar manner, trust without a *reason* for trusting is not trust. The small boy, like the man, must use every method available to compare authorities on nonverifiable matters, and to compare

[1] William Temple, *Nature, Man and God.* London, 1934, p. 19 *note.*

their findings with his own as he grows more sensitive. His conclusions are not certainly true, but neither are his conclusions thus reached on a par with the conclusions reached by the tossing of a coin. Thus reasonable use of authority does not give us absolute certainty, but it seems to be the glory of man to live by faith rather than by that which is beyond doubt.

It cannot be said too strongly that the kind of authority of which we are now speaking is not the authority of infallibility. Indeed, an authority cannot be infallible and remain an *authority*. We get complete certainty only in the area of mathematics and logic, a certainty based ultimately on tautology. It is infallibly true that the number four, when squared, gives us sixteen, but that is because this was already part of what we meant by sixteen. Such certainty cannot come in nonmathematical conclusions, but we are forced to rely, instead, on *reliability*. But what more may we reasonably ask? We want to find those to whom we can turn in a mood of trust because they have shown themselves trustworthy.

There are very few of our human contacts in which we expect infallibility or anything like it. If I go to a physician and he diagnoses my case, I realize it is in one sense a guess, but I have reason to suppose his guess is far better than mine. My conviction is strengthened by the sight of his diploma on the wall, the books in his study, and his obvious acceptance by his medical colleagues. I know that the license to practice is taken away from the grossly incapable or untrustworthy. That this is what we seek in religion has been well said by Professor Horton:

> What the inquiring layman really hopes to find in his religious authority is not inerrancy, but the same kind of competence and reliability, based upon knowledge, skill, and experience, which he finds in his physician or his legal adviser.[2]

The chief trouble with the conception of religious authority of the past has been the failure to understand *spiritual* authority. Men have looked too often for a completely external and inerrant standard, not unlike a scientifically determined unit of measurement. The old categories of necessity and probability are not sufficient for the realm of spirit, though they do suffice in pure logic, the former applying to the general field of deduction and the latter to the field of induction. We must have a new category in the realm of the spirit, a category utterly different from either necessity or

[2] Walter M. Horton, "Authority without Infallibility," in *Religious Realism,* ed. by D. C. Macintosh, New York, 1931.

probability. It is the category of *trust*. If I have found in one or two instances that a man writes in such a way or acts in such a way that he speaks to my deepest self, I trust him as a guide to truth and have confidence in his insights. It would be preposterous to call this induction. The sampling process is so meager that we should not be justified in making any inferences on the basis of it, and it is equally preposterous to call it deduction because we have no certainty, in the strict sense, that the conclusions depended upon are true. In the realm of spirit, when dealing with persons, we introduce a new method, the method of *confidence*.

We begin to see, then, a possible key to the solution of the dilemma with which this chapter began. The parallel was pointed out between the problem of authority and the problem of induction and we may suspect that our vivid sense of the dilemma of authority has arisen largely from the analogy, even when not explicitly stated. We escape the horns of the dilemma by a better understanding of the nature of "trust" and by the realization that the tasks of life must be faced in the midst of constant tension between outside authority and inner conviction. We discover what pattern of life to follow, not by mere self-reliance and not by mere dependence, but by a thrust and counter-thrust of these two factors.

The authority on which we depend, in part, is of two kinds: that of the superior individual and that of the group. We are increasingly conscious today that we depend, not only upon the general mass of human experience (the authority of the race), but also upon the authority of the expert, the single gifted or trained individual. That this is true in science is illustrated by the fact that not one person in a million goes through for himself the experiments upon which some of the most advanced conclusions concerning the nature of the physical world are based. If the few experts were to band together to give the rest of us false information, we should not detect it, but we feel justified in trusting them not to deceive us deliberately.

The authority of the expert is also widely accepted in the field of the arts. The wide vogue of magazines which criticize and evaluate works of art and literature is a witness to our dependence on this type of authority. The literary critic is supposedly a person of more refined taste than most of us, and we therefore follow his judgment though not slavishly. We do not follow his judgment as though he were infallible, for we know that he may be wrong, but we also know that the burden of proof is upon us when we differ from the known expert. My conception of music might be a sounder one than that of a great producing musician, but the odds are against me.

If we follow authority so much in the other areas of life, why should we not follow it in the area of spiritual religion? The conditions would not seem to be so different and there is no doubt about the occurrence of spiritual experts. Though all men have in them capacities for divine companionship these capacities have certainly been more developed in some than in others. There are men who have undergone training in the religious life as rigorous as that necessitated in scientific training. If from the latter there emerges a Newton, it is reasonable to expect a genuine seer to emerge from the former. It is curious to reflect how often we have expected to receive answers to our religious questions from those who are not qualified to know since they have not deliberately opened themselves to the cultivation of the spiritual life. If we discover that there are men who have devoted themselves long and faithfully to the understanding of the spiritual life, it is as reasonable to follow their lead as to accept in botany the leadership of a man whose whole life has been devoted to the study of plants. Indeed, we may be justified in accepting the authority of the expert in religion more than that of the expert in science, for scientific theories change remarkably through the years while the elements of the religious attitude toward the world remain the same. The words of Micah about the essentials of religion are as valid now as when they were spoken, but the scientific theories of Micah's day have not been accepted as valid for centuries. The true prophet reaches down to a solid rock on which any and all spiritual religion is built and his devotional life no more goes out of date than lyric poetry goes out of date. Our knowledge of the internal world has about it an enduring quality that our knowledge of the external world does not have.

Our second source of authority is the group, and this is far more important than the lone expert. We do not live to ourselves alone and the practical test we usually make in any problem is the test of group judgment. If an individual finds that all of his fellows think him insane, it may be that he should continue to follow the path he has chosen, but he should do so in fear and trembling for the odds are greatly against him.

The test of the group is what we mean by the authority of the Church. The Church is the whole body of spiritually-minded men in all ages, and the individual is immensely strengthened by membership in it. Our modern life suffers greatly from its excessive contemporaneity, and anything which can make us sensible of a tradition for righteousness is a great source of power. We can be genuinely sorry for the person who does not know what it is to *belong*. It is thoroughly possible to feel this is one particular sect without thereby becoming uncatholic in our sympathies.[3] We may be conscious of a family tradition without despising other men, and we may be conscious of a particular church tradition without despising other churches. There must be a division of labor in religion as in industry, and a strong sense of denominational loyalty is not incompatible with spiritual religion provided other loyalties are understood and respected.

In our day there is a great shift in the direction of Catholicism and this shift is, on the whole, in the right direction. This tendency has given countless men a new sense of the reality of history and has made the "communion of saints" a live doc-

[3] Thus a man may feel a thrill as he looks at a stern New England meetinghouse and recognizes the tradition to which both he and his ancestors belong, but this does not mean that he fails to appreciate Durham Cathedral and that for which it stands.

trine. We see in religious worship a hopeful rejection of mere individualism and a keen recognition of our continuity with "all the saints who from their labors rest." The only danger of the Catholic movement is that it tends to be insufficiently Catholic and to omit many of the genuine saints. It is true that a Catholicism which includes *everything* becomes meaningless, and the line has to be drawn somewhere. There is a city of this world as well as a city of God, but the danger is that our limits shall be arbitrarily drawn. In any case, there is a radical error in any ecclesiastical system which makes it impossible to include John Woolman among the genuine "saints."

There has been a danger, at times, among the exponents of spiritual religion that they would renounce authority completely and hold that pure religion is nothing but the immediate contact between the individual soul and God. This has been a gross misunderstanding of the main stream of spiritual religion. But this error is not to be overcome by the simple process of accepting current Catholicism, either "Roman" or "Anglican." What we all seek is genuine Catholicism, stripped of modifiers, so that no clear insight into the meaning of life is ruled out in advance because of its *source*.

Spiritual religion has always encouraged a certain dependence upon individual guidance, a sense of which often comes in times of private devotion. This keeps religion from being a second-hand affair, but then arises the problem, how is the individual to know when he is in the right? If we say that the only test is for each to follow his own "inner light," that is tantamount to the recognition that no test is possible. Are we not, then, in a position in which we are forced to uphold every queer person who says he is following his own inner light? How shall we distinguish between the prophet and the fanatic?

Though it has long been recognized in practice, we have been slow in theory to recognize how largely this problem of individual guidance is solved by the experience of group life. In some religious circles it has been common for the individual who believes he is led by the Spirit to subject his "leading" to the prayerful consideration of the circle of friends to which he belongs. In all generations there has been a sense in which the local congregation has been the real religious unit. Some groups have worked out a remarkably successful technique in which an effort is made to arrive at a group decision. Sometimes conclusions are reached by the entire company which are not identical with conclusions reached by any individuals before entering into the venture in group guidance. If the group cannot come to a decision at once, it is sometimes able to do so after a period of silent waiting. The crucial point is that the problem is not faced in the mood of the debating club nor is it considered as a matter for the intellect alone.

The search for new light is entered into by those who attempt to be members one of another and who seek light in the spirit of reverence. It should be understood that the word "group" is here used in a specialized sense. By a group is meant a fairly small company of persons already having enough in common to start thinking and seeking together without embarrassment. A large company, of several hundred or more, cannot be expected to carry on group thought or seek group guidance. Most of us have little circles of which we are integral parts and to which we can submit our deepest decisions. In the general experience of the race, group life has been as real as individual life, but we have often failed to take advantage of the fact.

Group life becomes for many a reality in the experience of worship, but if we are to accept the notion of a worship that covers all of existence, we may expect the same kind of group experience in common decisions. What should the individual do if the guidance of the group differs from his own? It would be dangerous to say that he should always give up his own conviction, for history has shown that the lone individual is sometimes right. The individual should ask the group to help him with his problem and should try to become part of the group as the matter is considered. He may find that he is still convinced of what is truth for him, though the group does not agree, and then he must go forward according to the light he sees, but always in great humility.

One of the best examples of how the individual may be conscious of his group life and yet resolute in his own path is seen in the decision of John Woolman to go to England on a religious visit. Before he went he presented his "concern" to his fellows at home and they agreed that it was right for him to go. Several thought he should go as comfortably as possible, but his mind was not easy in the cabin with its superfluity of decoration, so, in much discomfort, he went in the steerage. When he arrived in England the Londoners were somewhat condescending to the rural-looking New

Jersey tailor and it was the considered judgment
of the group to which he went that he should return home without delivering his message. Woolman was much saddened by this decision, and told
his religious guests that he would not be a burden
to them since he knew a trade, but he did not feel
free to return home. In other words, Woolman
acquiesced in the decision of the group in one way
and yet not in another. He differed from the group
almost in fear and yet he could not be untrue to
the truth as he saw it. His individualism was se-
verely limited and he did not disregard the rights
of others. It is almost needless to say that Woolman's mixture of submissiveness and strength of
character was so appealing that the whole group
was mellowed and asked him to go forward at
once with his message.

We see, then, that the problem of authority
introduces us to the fact of tension. There is
something finer than submission to authority and
something finer than mere dependence on inner
guidance. If inner leading and outer authority are
kept in a state of constant tension as they were in
the classic experience of John Woolman, we shall
have a perfect technique for spiritual living. We
must receive help from every quarter which offers

it, from the Bible, from the tradition of the Fathers, from the group, but, after we have had all the help we can get, we must still go forward in the light of God's truth as directly revealed in our hearts.

XI. The Abolition of the Laity

In all developed spiritual religion the ministry
occupies a large place. The task of the minister is
rightly looked upon as a sacred one, for the minister attempts nothing less than the effort to make
the presence of God more real to men. The minister intends to act as guide and friend, fanning
into a flame the embers of faith that are found
in each human soul. The minister's job is to stab
the spirits of men awake, to remind them of their
high calling, and to stimulate every good desire.
In each human heart there is something akin to
God, a Seed which may be lying dormant, and
the purpose of the minister of the spirit is to
nourish and cultivate that Seed until it comes to
flower. The act of cultivation may include the
attempt to stifle and destroy much that is evil.
Our conception of the ministry derives directly
from our conception of the spiritual nature of
man.

The most important way in which the minister can nourish the Seed of God in men is through the experience of worship. Worship is the highest and holiest experience possible for men, and they cannot but be lifted to new levels if they are taught to share in this experience. The primary task of the minister, then, is that of the development of a mood of worship on the part of himself and others. If he can speak ever so wisely and well and yet cannot stimulate the latent tendencies to worship, found in all men, he has failed in large measure.

The point we are making may be further clarified by saying that the task of the minister is almost identical with that of the poet. A poet is one who takes the fragmentary insights of ordinary men and builds them into a patterned whole so that they give delight. All of us are full of half-expressed, half-understood thoughts and feelings about the mysterious world that surrounds us, but we are baffled because we cannot bring these fragments to completion. The poet does for us what we want to do and cannot do alone. Wordsworth said poetry was emotion recollected in tranquillity, and all agree that the statement has a large element of truth. We can say, likewise, that the minister is one who, in the tranquillity of the hour of worship, helps other men to recollect and ennoble the scattered bits of true emotion which they have had at other times as they have contemplated life's mystery.

There is in the world a vast amount of near-religion. Many who speak little of God and perhaps say they do not believe in Him, indicate in numerous ways that they have had in their own lives responses to life's mystery that are remarkably similar to the responses of saints and prophets. In the same way many persons who profess to have nothing but disdain for poetry show plainly when they are off their guard that they, too, see meaning and beauty as well as sticks and stones. Often a real poet can make such people appreciate their latent poetic feelings when they could not do so alone. The minister must likewise bring together the religious elements in men's lives and dignify them by relating them to God.

How strange it is that prophets and priests and poets can help us! We might easily suppose either that a man has a sense of God, in which case help is not needed, or that he has no sense of God, in which case there is nothing to which appeal can be made. This apparent dilemma is similar to the one concerning the teachability of virtue to which Plato gives his famous answer in the *Meno*. Our answer is really the same as his, and this is not surprising, for the debt of spiritual religion to Plato is immense. The sense of God *is* already in us, but we need help to come to a full realization of it. We need a spiritual guide to do for us what Socrates did for the slave who was ignorant of mathematics. The paradox is that we can only become our true selves through great effort and through external aid.

It is because of the paradox just mentioned that preaching is not in vain. We have high hopes and we make great resolves, but we tend to forget and *we need to be reminded of what it is that we really want.* The ways in which we are reminded of our true selves and thus helped to "come to ourselves" are multitudinous, and that is why the ministry should be as wide as the world.

The minister must be a genuine prophet, speaking directly to the conditions of men, guided more by their needs than by his preconceived ideas. He must try to find the real desires for good which men already have, though they may be dormant, and appeal to these. He must be, to adapt the phrase of Socrates, a "spiritual midwife" who helps men to bring reverence to birth.

The ideal sermon is one which arises out of the mood of worship and, at the same time, enhances the mood of worship. The sermon should enter

THE ESSENCE OF SPIRITUAL RELIGION

the stream and enhance its movement, as is done by the motor-driven water wheels we see in amusement parks. When this is done the worshiper has no sense of wrench or jar and yet he is carried to levels he little expected to reach. We frequently hear a sermon which sounds profound and yet is a total failure because it is delivered in the mood of the classroom. It reminds us of the study rather than of the altar rail, and we suspect that it was written quite apart from any thought of the present congregation. A sermon cannot reach the level which spiritual religion demands unless the preacher is continuously sensitive to the needs of those about him, so that he is ready to shift either subject matter or emphasis on a moment's notice. The true minister is not simply one who comes to the hour of worship with a finished product; he is one who continues to the end of his discourse in his openness to the leadings of the Holy Spirit.

Does this seem too high a standard? It is a high standard, but we must remember that the minister is engaged in a holy task and no effort is too great. If the minister is continually responsive to his people and their needs he may often be forced to abandon the sermon he has prepared with such care and speak out of the fullness of his heart. If he has the courage to do so, and if his product seems less polished, he may nevertheless discover that the needs of others have been met as they could never be met by a merely polished discourse.

What topics are suitable for such ministry that is akin to poetry and that seeks to enhance the mood of worship? The topic must be one which arouses a sense of wonder or of love and must not be merely a matter of cold information. Above all, it must not be controversial. There is plenty of room for controversy in the world and the mood of the debating society has its place, but it is absolutely destructive of the mood of worship. We must use material that draws men together into an organic unity, making them conscious of the deep things that unite them rather than of the issues which divide them, many of which are superficial and temporary.

The best material for sermons comes from glimpses into common life which show its unsuspected depth or glory. We should use scenes or incidents from life or literature which make people realize something of the meaning which lies beneath the crass surface. When sermons use this material they are genuinely catholic in that they may eventually reach *all* men. The danger is that we shall be partisan rather than catholic, and we are partisan when we discuss special causes or attempt to promote specific legislation. A sermon on the "child spirit" is more catholic than one on the United Nations. One great advantage of Biblical texts is the fact that the Bible is so far away from us in time that its messages cease to be partisan and take on the character of complete universality.

This does not mean that the minister must avoid entirely any reference to practical life, lulling his people to sleep with pious and beautiful words while men about them are suffering. It does mean, however, that we shall make men most able to face with intelligence and love the practical problems of ordinary living if we help them to come at these very problems from the mood of high worship. Men can solve their problems best if they are not close to them all the time; they need perspective, and this is what worship provides. The task of economic readjustment can be better attacked by one who has refreshed his spirit through a recognition of the things which endure.

Thus far, in this chapter, we have considered the ministry as though it were the task of a few men. This is the usual assumption, but is this assumption a sound one? If we consider carefully our basic premises of spiritual religion we soon realize that they entail the breakdown of any hard and fast distinction between the clergy and the laity. If every human being has in him something akin to God, and if revelation is continuous, why may not *any* child of God become a minister in the sense that he helps to cultivate and nourish the Seed of God in others? Indeed, if we define a minister as one who thus nourishes the Seed, we soon realize that we have known hundreds of ministers who were not such officially and we have known many others who, in spite of clerical garb and ordination, were not ministers at all. Much of the best ministry in the world has been unconscious ministry. All of us can remember with thanksgiving certain unknown and unsung persons who, by words or silence, have stirred up our own latent sense of God's presence, and have thus made worship real for us.

The Christian religion, especially, leads straight to the abolition of the laity. The whole spirit of Jesus led his followers beyond the kind of faith in which some men were priests, and he seemed to take a particular delight in showing how the ministry of the nonpriest might exceed that of the man to whom had been assigned a priestly function. Witness, for example, the Good Samaritan.

It is instructive to note that the immediate followers of Jesus had the ideal of a universal priesthood and they must have caught it from their Master. It was expected that fishermen should preach, and so many shared in the ministry at Corinth that St. Paul had to give suggestions for the right conduct of the meeting.[1] The point is that St. Paul did not make the suggestion, which would certainly occur to a modern Christian, that they appoint one man and let him be the preacher for the others. At two places in one New Testament book the ordinary Christians are called a priesthood, either holy or royal.[2] Here was a new order; the old system was overcome, not by destroying its priesthood, but by enlarging it to include all devout souls.

Though the early standard was not maintained in the Church, it is still valid. A full understanding of the Christian message leads us straight to the position that all Christians are ministers and that the mere layman is nonexistent. There may be some division of labor in this generalized ministry, as St. Paul explained, but we must not

[1] I Corinthians 14.
[2] I Peter 2:5, 9.

suppose that a division of labor necessarily entails a difference in rank or honor. There may be diversities of gifts, but there is the same Spirit.

The great ideal of the abolition of the laity has caught hold of men fitfully, but it has never been seriously followed in the Church at large, at least not since the first Christian century. Sometimes the cleavage has been so marked that one kind of doctrine has been held suitable for the priests who know and another has been taught to the common man. This is dangerous on the grounds of sincerity, if on no other, and certainly finds no counterpart in the teaching of Jesus. Spiritual religion is a religion of *veracity* and is willing to run the risks of truthtelling. If an educated minister does not believe in a physical hell, he is undermining the very foundation of faith when he proceeds to preach such a hell to his supposedly ignorant hearers. The abolition of the laity involves an abolition of a double standard of truth and a double standard of morality. The "hard sayings" of Jesus, which we find especially in the Sermon on the Mount, are shorn of their power if we interpret them as applicable to the priesthood and not to the common man. That is too easy a way out of the difficulty and spiritual religion cannot take it.

The notion of a universal priesthood has broken out in many strange places in the history of the Church, thus showing that there is something about the nature of the Christian message which will not let men rest content with an easy acceptance of a two-level order. Among ordinary Christians there have long been practices which tend, in reality, to deny a sharp cleavage between clergy and laity, in spite of what they say.[3] The practice of family prayer is a case in point. Countless Christian parents have been priests and priestesses at their own firesides, as have Hebrew parents for so many generations.

The ideal of the abolition of the laity came near to concrete embodiment at the time of the Reformation. Martin Luther envisaged the ideal for a time and made it his battle cry when he spoke of "the Priesthood of the Believer," but he seems to have made no serious attempt to put it into practice. As a matter of fact most Christians, unless their attention is called to this high ideal, consider that a few are ministers while most are not, and they mean by a minister a person who has had theological training or has had

[3] A full account of such outbreakings will be found in Rufus M. Jones' two volumes, *Studies in Mystical Religion* (London, 1908) and *Spiritual Reformers in the Sixteenth and Seventeenth Centuries* (London, 1914).

the rite of ordination. When we consider the question we quickly realize that this conception of the ministry is amazingly artificial. A man might go to a dozen theological schools and be well versed in Church History, and yet not be a person at all able to cultivate and arouse the spirit of worship in ordinary men. He might not even *care* to cultivate and arouse this spirit. The same can be said of any ceremonial act, such as ordination, with or without the laying on of hands. It is hard to see how the prophetic spirit can be inherited or passed on by mechanical arrangement. What we want, then, in spiritual religion is a conception of the ministry that accords with reality and is not merely a matter of externals that cannot possibly change the inner spirits of men.

How shall men prepare for the ministry so conceived? A knowledge of the Bible and religious history will undoubtedly help, but the point is that such knowledge alone is not *sufficient*. We must get help from every angle to make us more conversant with the spirit of man and we must keep ourselves tenderly open to new recognitions of human need. Above all, we must keep ourselves open to new leadings, new messages which we believe are the direct inspiration of God who is Spirit. We must face our ministry, not in a dull or prosaic way, but in a mood of expectancy, and in a mood of prayer. This has been well said by a modern exponent of spiritual religion, in consideration of the place of reflective thought and factual information in the prophet's mind.

He may, indeed, go through all this preparation of thought, but the essential preparation for his work is prayer; prayer in which he must be willing to lay aside, if need be, all these thoughts of this. The prophetic spirit reaches out to realize the condition of those to whom it is to minister, and upward in search of light and strength from its only source.[4]

If we enter our ministry with a lively sense of the sacredness of persons and of the reality of continuous revelation, we shall not be surprised if we are given new light that will aid us in reaching the lives of other men and stirring up the divine tendencies in them.

The ministry demanded in a really spiritual religion is as wide as the world. There is the ministry of common labor, of teaching, of bringing health. If we could see our daily tasks as part of the ministry, if we could know that what we do is valuable only as it helps in some way to arouse the sense of God's Presence, then all life

[4] T. Edmund Harvey, *A Wayfarer's Faith*. London, 1920, p. 36.

would be infinitely raised. We might do the same things as before, but they would be ennobled because they would be part of a world-wide ministry of the spirit.

This larger sacerdotalism does not involve the fantastic notion of the equality of all men. Just as some men are superior to others as artists or scientists, so it is reasonable to suppose that some men are superior to others as guides of the human spirit. There may be a difference in capacity, just as there is a division of labor, and we shall certainly continue to turn to those who have proved their ability to help us, but we can all belong to the same profession even though not all are equally adept at it. We all renounce crawling, even though some of us walk poorly, and spiritual religion calls on men to abolish the laity, even though their efforts in the ministry may be feeble. In time, such a change in the thought of our vocation is sure to affect our practice.

XII. The Implications of Reverence

Spiritual religion, rightly conceived, will never be an escape from life into a private Holy of Holies where the individual is selfishly concerned with his own spiritual state. The person who accepts the notion of the sacrament of common life will, indeed, have his Holy of Holies to which he retires, but his experience there will make him more sensitive to human wrongs rather than lull him into a mood of apathetic resignation. He finds on every hand outright denials of human brotherhood and his deep conviction concerning the spiritual nature of man as man makes it impossible for him to share in these denials.

The chief problem in the development of spiritual religion lies not in getting people to accept its fundamental insights, but in making them consider carefully what the acceptance of these premises must eventually involve. For example, it has

THE IMPLICATIONS OF REVERENCE

been common for war to be defended and yet these insights accepted. Since God is love, it is argued, we must stop forces in the world which make for strife, i.e., our national enemies; and since souls alone are sacred, since there is "that of God in every man," we must destroy those who are not respecting the sacredness of human life. It would not be hard to collect many pronouncements from eminent men in which this particular logic or lack of logic is illustrated.

But let us consider a little more carefully what these propositions really entail. In the first place, if God is one eternal Spirit, completely loving, and if we are akin to Him, even remotely, it is our high destiny to be loving, too. Jesus expressed the character of God by the use of the happy figure "Our Father," and it follows that children of the same Father are brothers. We must be brothers, then, not only of those who are being wounded, but also of those who are doing the wounding. In the second place, if each man, regardless of appearances, has in him spiritual potentialities, it follows that each human life, irrespective of nationality, is sacred. The life of the enemy soldier is sacred just as truly as is the life of the friendly civilian.

It must be admitted that religion has frequently

been so separated from life that men have shed tears at the thought of Christ's sufferings while they have hardly noticed the sufferings of their fellow men. The sacraments of the Church can be, when wrongly used, escapes from ordinary living. In the words of a former principal of Ruskin College, Oxford:

It is an amazing and anomalous thing that people are found to give so much reverence to the bread and wine of the altar and yet so little regard to the flesh and blood of their brothers "for whom Christ died," and of whom he said, "Inasmuch as ye do it unto one of the least of these ye do it unto me." I would not ask anyone to give up a sacrament or ritual that he or she finds to be a helpful means of grace and inspiration. I would only ask that we should all expect to find the "Real Presence" in unexpected times and places and especially that we should give a reverence and devotion to the flesh and blood of our fellows no less than to the bread and wine of the altar, that we should feel a sense of the sacredness of human life and personality, and recognize war and poverty and disease for the blasphemies they are.[1]

Just as we tend to reduce the sacraments to a few conventional symbols we also tend to reduce blasphemy to conventionally sinful words. It takes only a little reflection to make us realize that the real blasphemy comes in action, and that a man

[1] A. Barratt Brown, *Wayside Sacraments*. London, 1932, p. 12.

144

may be a terrible blasphemer though his remarks about God, Christ, and the Bible are scrupulously correct. It is infinitely worse to crush a man, who is a Temple of the Holy Spirit, than to chip a piece of stone from an altar. When we create slums we are helping to profane God's House, no matter what we may say in church.

One of the strange and discouraging features of human life is the strong tendency men have to try to uphold their own dignity by refusing to accept others on a basis of equality. This is particularly true when groups of men differ in some obvious, though relatively unimportant fashion, such as skin color. In many parts of the world white men, for example, refuse to extend genuine brotherhood to their fellow men of dark color. Men find themselves shut out from cultural opportunities and forced to avoid certain areas, not because they have done any wrong and not because they are ill-bred, but merely because they belong to a different race from the race which happens to be dominant.

What is the cure for this spirit which constantly wounds sensitive natures? The cure is a recognition of the truth that every human being is a child of God, made in God's image, and with a Seed of God in him. We cannot deliberately

THE ESSENCE OF SPIRITUAL RELIGION

wound a person whom we really consider a Temple of the Holy Spirit. The cure lies in taking the spiritual view of man, of trying to look at men as souls, to look beyond their bodies. After all, the souls of black and brown people are remarkably the same as the souls of white people, and this we can know for sure when the submerged people become articulate in literature and art. We find, then, that they are equally capable of love, of hate, of great faith, and of mental anguish.

If we come to think of any human being with reverence, not so much for what he is as for what he may become, we can never again put up artificial barriers to make life harder for any. Life is hard enough, anyway, in view of the dangers to health and the continual economic struggle, but for a large portion of mankind we deliberately erect barriers to make life harder. A full recognition of "that of God in every man" makes the barriers crumble and leads us to try to make opportunities for the full flowering of what is potential in other men, no matter how different from us they may seem.

We can never despise another human soul without at the same time making a mark on our own souls. Just as we are lifted and made new by ad-

146

miration and worship, we debase ourselves when we exhibit irreverence in the presence of what is potentially holy. Hatred is a terrible thing and its worse effects are seen in the life of the person who allows himself to indulge in the hatred.

There is no tragedy like that of the potential which is denied actuality. Consider, let us say, a child who has in him a great capacity as a musician, so that with the right help at the right time he could become a perfected artist, a source of joy to himself and to others. What if he never meets the person who takes an interest in him and has the ability to give him a start on this high road? We know that those who have reached great heights have not done so by their own efforts alone, but that always there has been someone to give the necessary aid. There must be many persons in the world who are now living stunted lives when they have had *capacities* as great as the capacities of others who have grown beautifully. If we have normal human feelings, and if we have reverence for human potentialities, we cannot consider such a situation without being profoundly stirred.

It is the deep faith of spiritual religion that there is in all men a divine Seed, but that Seed cannot nourish itself. That in us which is akin to

God *can* remain dormant and always needs someone to help with the germination. The Christian
dedicates himself to this holy task. He attempts
to go to whatever place on the globe has the greatest need of such nourishers of the Seed. He sees
no reason why he should minister to his own group
alone and disregard those on other continents.
In like manner he sees no reason why he should
limit himself to so-called cultural pursuits and
overlook the changes that are needed economi-
cally. The ultimate blasphemy often comes because the conditions of living are such that the
Seed has no chance from the first.

As we look over the human scene we observe
that the differences in opportunity are immense.
A few of us in Europe and those parts of the
globe most influenced by Europeans have almost
everything at our command that we could wish.
We are within easy reach of excellent medical
attention, we have abundant opportunities for
education, we are surrounded by books, and we
have machines which eliminate a vast amount of
routine labor. Of course we have our own forms
of misery, but when we compare our lot with
the lot of the so-called backward peoples or even
our own neighbors we are really amazed at the
contrast.

There are large areas which have almost none of the things which make our lives rich and interesting and, in addition, we have even spoiled the system of life these other peoples once had. We have drained off their wealth to make our vaunted progress possible and, in so doing, have given the backward peoples diseases which they did not have before.

Considerations like those mentioned above make it clear that a really spiritual religion is at once a *social* religion and a *missionary* religion. If we *care* about the souls of men, especially when these men are less favored than ourselves, we cannot sit idly by while they are denied those things which would make their lives finer and which we could provide. Indeed, if we admit that part of the evil condition of others is the price that has been paid for the things we enjoy, we are not benevolent when we work for them, but are merely paying a debt long overdue. If a missionary goes to other peoples with a patronizing and condescending air, if he goes to tell them that the things they prize are necessarily worse than the things we prize, he is not looking on human souls with the reverence and wonder which spiritual religion demands. The truly spiritual missionary goes out, not primarily in the interest of a system of teaching, but in the interest of men. He cares for persons; he is wounded in his own spirit when they are denied those things which will develop their sacred and latent powers. He is not so much trying to save them from hell as to save them in the absolute sense discussed in an earlier chapter. He finds men everywhere who are unsaved, i.e., *wasted,* and he cannot accept this situation without action on his part.

The solution of the missionary problem, as is true of so many other problems, lies in the attitude of "not less but more." There is a type of missionary activity which spiritual religion is bound to oppose, but we oppose it best by adopting a larger and more inclusive point of view which makes missionary work as wide as the world. It is a great mistake to divide the world into our lands and the mission field, but the remedy does not lie in giving up the missionary concept; the remedy lies in so enlarging the mission field that it includes our own land as well as others.

If we could make the world our field and if every profession could be undertaken in a missionary spirit, a new day would dawn for mankind. We can see grave evils at home as well as abroad, and we must attack all evils which in any way hinder the growth and development of the Divine Seed. If a missionary is one who nourishes the Seed in others, we need missionaries everywhere, and there is no more noble profession. This might take on many forms, such as medicine or politics or business, but all tasks would be equally noble providing they express human brotherhood and help in some way or other, no matter whether small or great, to break down the barriers which keep men back from the growth in life of which they are capable and to which they are divinely called. A nonmissionary Christian is a contradiction in terms. Just as Christianity, rightly understood, entails the abolition of the laity, it also entails the abolition of the nonmissionary class. It is obvious that what has just been said of missionary work applies equally to "social service." Here, also we must so enlarge the area that the field of endeavor becomes one.

Often the greatest barriers to brotherhood exist between people of the same race who live side by side, but without a recognition of equality on the part of the supposedly superior group. We see the beginnings of a caste system as between white-collar workers and manual laborers, and the growing child soon learns that there are people he just does not "meet." We get so accustomed to snobbishness that we seldom realize the scars it makes. It is hard enough to keep up one's self-respect in this world without having it deliberately battered down by others.

What does spiritual religion have to do with class distinction? Spiritual religion sees it as completely evil because it hinders and dwarfs the growth of "that of God in every man." Spiritual religion looks beyond the clothing, the occupation, the accent, the educational opportunities, and tries to see what the soul of the man is or may be or might have been.

Spiritual religion, in other words, involves a radical democracy. Democracy has always been adopted, when it has been adopted, as a great faith. It is a faith which may prove unfounded, and it is a faith which is often sadly shaken by the results, but it remains one of the major insights of rare souls that the common man can be depended upon if he is given a chance. This faith, essentially a mystical one, is the theme of most of the poetry of Walt Whitman. Whitman was a radical democrat because he found the same elemental human nature among the woodsmen of the far North, the slaves of the South, the women in their houses, and the statesmen at their desks. It is no wonder that this democratic faith became to Whitman a religion, for it is the necessary result of a fully developed religion.

Democracy grows out of reverence for human life. This does not mean that there must be a leveling down or that all men must be considered as actual equals in ability. They manifestly differ in physical strength, in mental alertness, as well as in opportunities. We need not maintain the fiction of equality when it does not exist, but this we must do: we must give every man the benefit of the doubt, we must put no artificial barrier in his way, we must provide an equality of opportunity. Unless we do have an equality of opportunity there will be many gifts which are never known because they have never been given the setting in which they could come to flower. Only by an equality of opportunity can we avoid the tragedy of waste, the waste of sacred human powers.

All this shows why it is that a spiritual religion is bound to affect our economic and social order. We begin with our reverence for the divine capacities in human life, we go on to see that we must break down all barriers which hinder the nourishment of the Seed, and we are thus forced to the conclusion that some economic and social systems are necessarily bad, for they involve the very barriers to fulfillment which must be broken down. Any system which makes the lives of some men mere pawns for the ambitions of others is absolutely and terribly evil and must eventually be destroyed. This is not the place to consider the details of the social order, but spiritual religion at least gives us our measuring stick in terms of which any order can be tested.

That system of life is good which sets men free, which releases divinely given powers, which provides for the nourishment of the spiritual life in all its phases. That system is evil which denies brotherhood and ceases to look on separate men as absolute ends, sacred in and of themselves. In conclusion we may say that a philosophical theory of the sacredness of personality will not be sufficient for the production of brotherhood. Our belief in the sacredness of human life must be transmuted into a powerful love which makes us break the chains which bind men because we really *care*. In this way we shall gain the power to know blasphemy when it appears and to go beyond it.

154

Index

Absolutism, 39
Addison, Joseph, 48, 49
Angels, 86
Apocalyptic teaching, 32, 33
Arnold, Matthew, 16, 19

Blasphemy, 144, 154
Bosanquet, Bernard, 64, 69
Brinton, Howard 83 n.
Brown, A. Barratt, 12, 96 n.

Carlyle, Thomas, 26
Ceremonialism, 34, 93
Child spirit, 48, 134
Cicero, 46, 47
Color vision, 101
Confidence, 117
Continuous revelation, 2, 101-103
Creative worship, 83
Creeds, 21, 35
Cumulative progress, 112, 113

Democracy, 153

Emerson, R. W., 30
Ethical legalism, 36
Eucharist, 92, 93

Fry, Joan M., 96 n.

Genetic method, 14, 15
Gothic architecture, 76
Gray, Thomas, 31
Group life, 124, 125

Harnack, A., 39 n., 61
Hartmann, N., 39 n.
Harvey, John W., 12
Harvey, T. Edmund, 96, 140 n.
Horton, W. M., 116

Ideal Spectator, 56, 57
Infallibility, 115
Inner Christ, 71, 72

Jones, Rufus M., 98 n., 138 n.

Lake, Kirsopp, 79
Lemmings, 62
Liberalism, 24
Longer Bible, 108
Lovejoy, Arthur O., 100 n.
Luther, Martin, 138

Magic, 41, 42
Materialism, 44, 45

155

INDEX

Matrimony, 68, 88
Missionary enterprise, 148, 149
Montaigne, 58
Morley, John, 14
Mormons, 106
Murray, Gilbert, 62

Otto, Rudolph, 15, 76

Patriotism, 68
Penn, William, 93
Penrose, J. Doyle, 93
Plato, 130, 131
Poetry, 7, 8, 16, 17
Pratt, J. B., 5
Prayer, 84
Prayer Book, 102
Priesthood, 138
Pringle-Pattison, A. Seth, 99 n.
Providence, 46-50

Racial antagonism, 145, 146
Reverence, 11-13
Roman Catholicism, 87, 108, 109, 121, 122
Royce, Josiah, 101, 102

Sabatier, A., 3, 4

Sacerdotalism, 141
Scholastic arguments, 50
Schweitzer, Albert, 39 n.
Scott, E. F., 33 n.
Seed of God, 128, 129, 135, 147, 148
Self-consciousness, 53-56
Shakers, 106
Shorter Bible, 108
Silence, 80, 81
Sin, sense of, 61
Socrates, 20, 63
Sperry, Willard L., 27
Stephen, Leslie, 22

Taylor, A. E., 51, 61
Temple, William, 15, 16, 114
Temples, 10, 11
Tolerance, 24, 25

War, 143
Westcott, Bishop, 39
Whitehead, Alfred N., 26
Whitman, Walt, 152
Whittier, John G., 27, 49
Woolman, John, 91, 122, 125, 126
Wordsworth, William, 129

75 76 77 78 10 9 8 7 6 5 4 3 2 1